Improving Social Behaviors In the Classroom

An Easy Curriculum for Teachers of Young Children with Autism, Developmental Disabilities and Typical Children

Curriculum:
Direct Teaching of Social Behaviors in the Classroom

Stephanny Freeman, Ph.D.,
Gazi Begum, M.A.,
Kristen Hayashida, M. Ed.,
and Tanya Paparella, Ph.D.

University of California, Los Angeles
Early Childhood Partial Hospitalization Program

Improving Social Behaviors in the Classroom
An Easy Curriculum for Teachers of Young Children with Autism,
Developmental Disabilities and Typical Children

Published by: DRL Books, Inc.
                  37 East 18th Street, 10th Floor
                  New York, NY 10003
                  Phone: 212-604-9637
                  Fax: 212-206-9329
                  www.drlbooks.com

Book Layout: Michelle Avedian and John Eng

Cover Art: Ramon Gil

Library of Congress Control Number: 2010924793
ISBN: 978-0-9755859-8-6

About the Authors

STEPHANNY F.N. FREEMAN, Ph.D.

Dr. Freeman is an Associate Clinical Professor in the Division of Child Psychiatry at UCLA, a licensed clinical psychologist, and Co-director of the Early Childhood Partial Hospitalization Program (ECPHP). She received her Ph.D. in Educational Psychology with a specialization in Special Education. As an elementary school teacher, she worked with children with autism and other exceptional children, designing individualized curricula and behavior plans. In graduate school, Dr. Freeman conducted assessments in a clinical environment, establishing expertise in cognitive, academic, language, and adaptive behavior instruments for children aged two to 18. Early research interests included social (peers and friendship) and emotional (recognition, empathy, and problem-solving) development. During a National Institute of Mental Health postdoctoral fellowship, she coordinated and carried out research-based intervention services for preschool children with autism.

Dr. Freeman directs the day-to-day activities of ECPHP staff and coordinates the evaluation, treatment, and development of appropriate multidisciplinary programs for school-aged and severely impaired children with autism. She assists parents in developing appropriate educational programs and school-based modifications, behavior education and training, and cognitive and social/emotional/play development. Current research areas include targeting core deficits and intervention, best-practice interdisciplinary interventions, and play/social skills development.

GAZI BEGUM, M.A.

Gazi Begum completed her undergraduate degree in psychology at the University of California, Los Angeles. After completing her B.A., she worked at the Early Childhood Partial Hospitalization Program for two years. Currently, Ms. Begum is a doctoral student in School Psychology at the University of California, Riverside. She is a recipient of the Doug Flutie Fellowship. Her research focuses on improving social and behavioral functioning of children with developmental disabilities through home-school partnerships. Ms. Begum also works at SEARCH, a family autism center that provides resources to low income and Spanish speaking families who have children with autism spectrum disorder.

KRISTEN HAYASHIDA, M.Ed.

Kristen Hayashida currently instructs and nurtures high-functioning children with autism at the University of California, Los Angeles, Early Childhood Partial Hospitalization Program (UCLA ECPHP). Serving as head teacher, she helps design and implement comprehensive treatment plans to improve her students' ability to function in the general education classroom and among their peers of conventional development. Additionally, Kristen is involved in research that examines co-occurring social and behavioral disorders in the clinic population of children with autism spectrum disorders. Kristen has also taught weekly social skills groups for young children with autism.

Kristen holds a Masters in Education from the Harvard Graduate School of Education in Human Development and Psychology. She graduated from UCLA with a bachelor's degree in Sociology with a minor in Applied Developmental Psychology.

Kristen's passion for underserved children with autism drives her to pursue novel ways to create social settings which allow them to participate in, and take advantage of, more mainstream programming for children.

TANYA PAPARELLA, Ph.D.

Dr. Paparella is an Assistant Clinical Professor in the Division of Child Psychiatry at UCLA and a licensed clinical psychologist. As Co-director of ECPHP, she is a specialist in the field of autism, having spent more than 15 years in intervention and research. Dr. Paparella received her master's degrees in Special Education and in Counseling Psychology from Rutgers University in New Jersey. Her formative years in applied autism intervention were spent at the Douglas Developmental Disabilities Center at Rutgers University where she designed, implemented, and evaluated educational programs. She received her Ph.D. in Educational Psychology from UCLA and completed a two-year National Institute of Mental Health postdoctoral fellowship in the Division of Child Psychiatry.

Dr. Paparella oversees the daily activities of ECPHP staff. She is actively involved in all aspects of the comprehensive evaluation and treatment of children with autism from 18 months to four years of age. She works closely with parents to support and educate them in all aspects of their child's treatment. Dr. Paparella provides ongoing clinical instruction for students, interns, and fellows from different specialties, and her research has focused on the development of core deficits in young children with autism. Her current clinical and research interests relate to the effectiveness of early intervention, particularly with respect to predictors of outcomes for toddlers on the autism spectrum.

Table of Contents

NOTE:
- **Each category has a topic for the week.**
- **Each week has a lesson plan for each day (Monday through Friday).**
- **Each week also contains "Generalization" and "Dear Parent" sections suggesting a few ways to generalize the activity during the school day and at home.**
- **The "Dear Parent" section can be copied and sent home at the start of the week.**

Introduction

How many preschool and early elementary school teachers of moderate to high functioning children with autism (and indeed, other children with developmental disabilities or even typical children) have observed tantrums, aggression, crying, whining, and other inappropriate behaviors if a child was not the "winner" or if a child ended up with the wrong color train? How many teachers have observed a child who takes items and is unable to share? How many teachers have observed children who constantly bump each other in line or are unable to maintain appropriate body space? Often, teachers use prompts, support, or correction either during or after the situation but find themselves constantly repeating these cues (e.g., "Give your friends space!") with some results but few tools to fall back on. Teachers have constantly reported to us that they need easy tools and lesson plans for classroom social behaviors with the intent to develop self-regulatory skills in the children.

Although a number of strong social programs exist (e.g., McKinnon & Krempa, 2002; Begun, 1995; Moyes, 2001), they are not necessarily tailored for a classroom setting with a busy teacher. Some may be less specific (i.e., not defining exactly what to do and say in a 'lesson') or more labor intensive than what a teacher with many students can manage; they may target activities for individual rather than classroom goals, focus on social skills in a home or community setting, or (and most frequently) are for children with higher level verbal skills. Even comprehensive books on children with autism primarily focus on out-of-school social groups, therapy targets, and peer programs.

This book focuses on social behaviors in the classroom: activities that help young children participate in the social environment of a classroom setting. As mentioned, these activities can be used by teachers of children in both general and special education settings.

In the Early Childhood Partial Hospitalization Program (ECPHP) at UCLA, we have created this systematic and developmental classroom social behaviors curriculum. The activities in this curriculum have not been tested in a randomized, control-group design and therefore this curriculum is not evidence-based. The structure and content, however, are based upon empirical research — which is not common in other classroom social curriculums. Indeed, Burns and Yesseldyke (2009) recently surveyed 174 special education teachers and 333 school psychologists to identify how frequently they were using evidence-based practice in their programs. Social skills training overall was used only about once a week but according to Forness and Kavale (2000), the mean effect size of a meta-analysis of social skill training programs was very small (.21), indicating a large gap between research and practice. Thus, most social skills training programs in schools are only used once a week and have scant evidence of effectiveness (empirical or evidence-based). Further, the selected social skills were arbitrary (not based on careful assessment or developmental pathways but on "what the children needed"). Anecdotally, we hear the same report. Professionals who come to our program regularly report using social skill activities but without consistency and without any sequence. They report frankly and honestly that they "grab" social skills activities as they find them or as they need them.

CHAPTER I

Theoretical Framework

Although this curriculum is not evidence-based, it is empirically derived and grows from an extremely strong body of evidence-based practice and philosophical frameworks.

The curriculum comes from a developmental/cognitive/behavioral approach.

We say "developmental" because skills build upon each other: mastery at one level of understanding allows for mastery at the next. The developmental ages provided are approximate and represent the average general range where the skill should be mastered and independent (i.e., without prompting or assistance from adults). The curriculum is a sequence of activities but teachers can choose their own starting points if they feel their students already possess the lower-level skills. We take our topics from research on play, joint attention, empathy, emotion recognition, perspective taking, and social skills that identify a broad developmental pathway.

We say "behavioral" because we use techniques known to work with children with autism: 1) Applied Behavior Analysis, which is the systematic application of behavioral principles to change student learning and behavior to a meaningful degree. 2) Discrete Trial Teaching, which involves breaking a skill into smaller parts, teaching one sub-skill at a time until mastery, allowing repeated practice in a concentrated period, providing prompting and prompt-fading as necessary, and using reinforcement procedures. 3) Direct Instruction, which combines focused, teacher-directed learning with sequenced, structured materials and high levels of student responding. These three methods of teaching have high effect sizes in meta-analytic reviews indicating strong evidence-based support (Leaf & McEachin, 1999).

We say "cognitive behavioral" because we incorporate the form of psychotherapy that emphasizes the important role of thinking in how we feel and what we do; that our thoughts cause our feelings and behaviors rather than the environment or other people. Thus the goal is to change our thoughts to control our own behaviors without having others play such a large role. Our techniques use questioning strategies, repetition, and guidance to change thinking; we focus on teaching the children *how* to change behavior as opposed to what to change. We use problem-solving questioning strategies and techniques, and a highly structured and goal-oriented curriculum. We use rational thinking and make the facts obvious in the situation such that children can identify these facts and use them in their strategies (Ellis, 1997; Beck, 2004).

Specific Empirically Based Strategies

- Dydactic Instruction ("This is how we share").

- Self-Instruction as a metacognitive strategy. Activities in this curriculum use self-talk and "catch phrases" for the children to use themselves to improve their performance and self-regulate. Students can use verbal statements that assist them in mediating a social situation (Graham, Harris, & Reid, 1992).

- Choral Responding. During this activity, teachers prompt students in a group to respond in unison at a brisk pace, thus dramatically increasing attentiveness and number of responses. Students are less likely to be off task, passively watch, or distract their peers because they are all busy answering questions (Heward, 1994; Heward et al., 1996).

- Errorless Learning. This involves a teacher embedding a correct response/prompt into a question, thus ensuring the student's correct response: because there is only one choice, there are fewer distractions, and children gain practice in responding correctly (Mueller, Palkovic, & Maynard, 2007).

- Sociodramatic Scripts. These are sometimes used to model the social skill (with props and puppets), allowing children the opportunity to practice the script, and prompting the use of the social skill when needed throughout the day (Guglielmo & Tryon, 2001).

- Effective Praise. Characteristics of effective praise include being contingent on desirable behaviors (Shores, Gunter, & Jack, 1993), behavior specific (Chalk & Bizo, 2004), and focused on effort and process (Dweck, 2000). Although definitions are mixed in the field, effective praise statements convey to children the specific social behaviors in which teachers would like to see them continue to engage — thus, they fit each situation specifically.

How do we know what to teach?

This was another concern that was constantly brought to our attention by the wonderful local public school teachers who came to our program to observe. They would tell us that they were teaching social skills in their classrooms. When we asked them, "How did you know what topic to choose?" they would answer, "Whatever the issue was that week — if kids were having a hard time sharing and it seemed like a group issue, we tried to teach them about sharing." Or, "I found a book on teaching social skills so I went through and found topics that seemed to apply to our class and then I tried to figure out a way to make it fit our class." Both are good strategies when there are no other options but neither takes into account the developmental levels of the children, the setting (often the social skill was appropriate for either home or community), or the social and behavioral standards that are expected of children of a particular age. If, for example, a particular child is not able to acknowledge or respond to peers, understand emotion, accept or give an object to a peer, then sharing is likely not an appropriate skill to teach.

The sequence in this curriculum was put together first using The Douglass Developmental Disabilities Center (2007) Curriculum Checklist. This was the broadest and most comprehensive of curriculums found. Then, using the Social Skills Rating Scale (Gresham & Elliott, 1990), and the Social Responsiveness Scale (SRS; Constantino & Gruber, 2005), two independent coders categorized each item and placed them within the Douglass Checklist. Percent agreement was 92%. Through discussion with a third coder, the last categories were sorted.

Children with autism do not develop social skills in the same developmental pathway that children with typical development do. Certain social skill development in children with autism is "different" and not "delayed" (VanMeter, Fein, Morris, Waterhouse, & Allen, 1997). The sequence that follows is developed from research on typical children and applied to the population of children with autism. It may be then, that some children in your classroom need a particular skill but have a higher level skill already in place. For example, a typical 18-month-old child can take a toy back and say, "That's mine" although he/she is not really ready to engage in a give and take interaction with a like peer. While a child with autism may not use language socially or assertively (even at age four) and requires assistance to express ownership of an item, he/she is able to interact with another child in a simple give and take interaction (rolling a ball back and forth). Thus it is necessary to pick and choose the appropriate curriculum given the needs of your classroom while taking into account the SKILL COMPONENTS necessary to carry out that activity. Each lesson in this curriculum lists the skill components that are required to carry out the activity. It is likely that any teacher who "knows" their children will be able to identify if the activity requires more than the child is able to participate in. The ages listed for each week's skill are the ages in which typical children generally have mastered the skill, not the age at which we should start teaching the child with autism.

Evidence Data From Early Childhood Partial Hospitalization Program

The ECPHP at UCLA is a laboratory environment, and data is collected on individual behaviors. Although the design is quasi-experimental, single subject data was collected on parent report of behavioral and social behavioral progress. We did not have unbiased or blind evaluators in the classroom, nor did many of the children have community teachers that were consistent pre- and post-program and as a result, we relied on parent report. We recognize a number of extraneous contributing factors (e.g., behavioral programs) but nonetheless all children participated in ECPHP with no other interventions at the time as the day was extremely intensive. Further, all of ECPHP behavioral programs are individualized but follow similar philosophies. Thus, the children's changes in behavior and social behavior could be attributed to the curriculum and interventions within ECPHP. Below, we present parent's behavioral ratings of their children before and after participating in the program (randomly chosen from those who participated).

The Achenbach & Rescorla (2000) Child Behavior Checklist 1 ½ - 5 years was used to evaluate pre- and post-program behaviors and social behaviors. Parents were asked to complete the scale when the child entered the program and at the end of the program. The CBCL/1 ½ - 5 obtains parents' ratings of 99 problem items plus descriptions of problems, disabilities, what concerns parents most about their child, as well as the best things about their child. Using a new national normative sample and larger clinical samples, the following cross-informant syndromes from the form were derived: Emotionally Reactive, Anxious/Depressed, Somatic Complaints, Withdrawn, Attention Problems, & Aggressive Behavior (this includes tantrums, defiance, frustration, selfish, and stubborn behaviors). Results are presented in T-Scores. Scores between 65 and 70 are in the Borderline Range while scores over 70 are in the Clinical Range.

Participant 1: Female

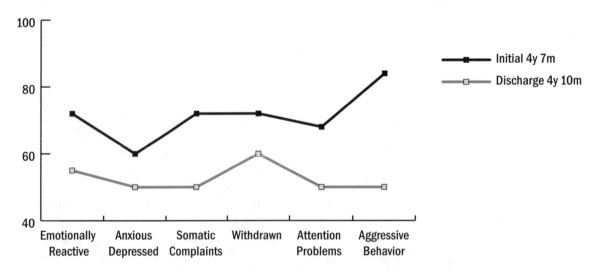

Parent quote: "My daughter's improved ability to regulate her behavior has been significant. We use 'be cool' so often and it makes complete sense to her. She even tells me while I'm driving, 'Remember Mommy, be cool!'"

Participant 2: Male

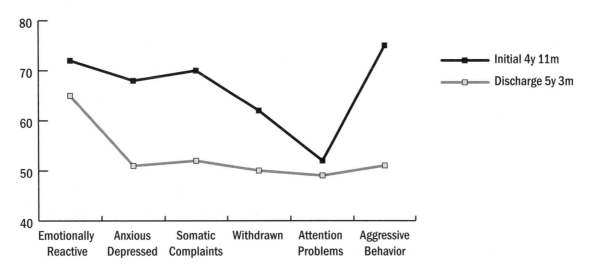

Parent quote: "Both 'be cool' and 'sometimes things are different' were constantly used in our home! We used to have to park our cars in the exact same order or he would tantrum. Now we just use the catch phrases and behavioral strategies taught by the teachers and he deals."

Participant 3: Male

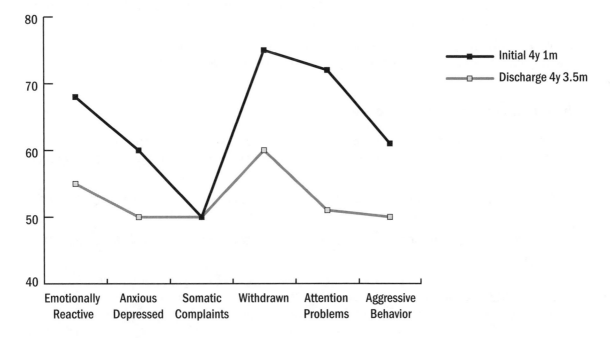

Parent quote: "Since our son transitioned to a mixed (special education and typical children's) preschool in the middle of the school year (February) from ECPHP, we made sure the teacher of the new program knew all the 'catch phrases' from this curriculum. We just made a list and gave them to her. She used them with our son and the first time she said, 'be strong' he looked at her like, 'how'd you know that?' and immediately adjusted his language volume and his body. His withdrawal from his social world lasted less than a second even in the new setting."

CHAPTER II

This curriculum, Direct Teaching of Social Behaviors in the Classroom, has worked best for children who have social and social language skills between the ages of 3-7. For example, many of our 7-8 year old high-functioning children with autism had social and social language skills that were more at a 3-4 year old level and thus were appropriate for the program.

The curriculum is:

- For preschool or early elementary special education teachers of children with autism, autism spectrum disorders, and/or children with other developmental and emotional difficulties.

- For preschool teachers of typically developing children.

- A user-friendly set of activities to carry out in small groups within a classroom structure.

- To be carried out by teachers or teachers' assistants in short periods of time but that can be revisited throughout the day.

- To be carried out in a manner that fits the needs of the group, the setting, and the environment of the classroom. It is the teacher's decision at what point within each category it is appropriate to begin and then each week can build upon the previous week.

- Flexible enough that teachers can choose to spend as much or as little time on a week's worth of lessons as appropriate for their classroom.

- Meant to be generalized so that teachers can use catch phrases throughout the curriculum week as well as throughout the year at other times, when appropriate.

The intent is to provide teachers with:

- A developmentally appropriate sequence of more basic social skills. The sequence utilizes the idea of "breaking down a skill into component parts" and provides the component parts to teach.

- An easy curriculum that is targeted and developmentally appropriate for young children with autism spectrum disorders or other developmental disabilities.

- A week's worth of activities within a particular social skill theme as well as generalization ideas.

- Activities that take into account the specific learning needs of younger children with autism. Most social skill programs demand higher levels of thinking, the skills are for children who have the basics, and they include complex language and activities.

The most important tips are:

- Adjust the language as you see fit given the language level of the students in the classroom. Simple is better.

- Use a strong voice, be very clear, and get to the point.

- Use the "catch phrases" frequently throughout the day.

Curriculum

**Direct Teaching of Social Behaviors in the Classroom:
An Easy Curriculum for Teachers of Young Children with Autism,
Developmental Disabilities, and Typical Children**

Category 1 | Possessive Understanding/ Acknowledgement of Others

■ **Week 1** **Assertiveness Over Ownership of Personal Items (18 months)**
Children will learn to express ownership verbally over their items and retrieve their personal belongings.

■ **Week 2** **Plays Near Another Child (24 months)**
Children will learn to play in close proximity to peers.

■ **Week 3** **Parallel/Aware Play (30 months)**
Children will learn how to onlook to their peers during play and use the information from a peer's play to inform their own play.

■ **Week 4** **Interacts With Other Children (30 months)**
Children will learn the basics of peer interaction skills.

■ **Week 5** **Expressive Ownership: Refuse/Retrieve Belongings (30 months)**
Children will learn to use polite and appropriate language to retrieve, hang onto, and share their personal belongings.

■ **Week 6** **Shows Displeasure Verbally Instead of Physically (42 months)**
Children will learn to express displeasure verbally and control negative emotions.

■ **Week 7** **Asserts Self in Socially Appropriate Ways (54 months)**
Children will learn to assert themselves in socially appropriate ways.

Week 1 Assertiveness Over Ownership of Personal Items
"That's Mine!"

Behavioral Objective

Children will learn to express ownership verbally over their items and retrieve their personal belongings.

Identify the Skill Components

- Recognition of a favorite toy as their own
- Language: verbalizing "That's mine!"
- Ability to retrieve belongings
- Care for personal belongings
- Ability to pass items to peers

Lessons and Materials for the Week

Day	Lesson	Materials
Monday	Mix It Up	Favorite toy from home
Tuesday	Scoot to Your Toy	Favorite toy from home, scooter board
Wednesday	Run to Your Toy	Favorite toy from home
Thursday	Monster Attack	Favorite toy from home, monster puppet
Friday	Slide to Your Toy	Favorite toy from home, slide structure (outdoor)

NOTE:

This week's lessons all involve the child's personal possessions from home.
Be sure to ask parents to bring in the materials listed above in advance.

For the Parents

Dear Parents,

This week, our social skill classroom behavior is:

Category 1: Possessive Understanding/Acknowledgment of Others	
Week 1	Assertiveness Over Ownership of Personal Items "That's Mine!"

Many children do not assert themselves when something belongs to them or if something is taken away from them. It is important for us to help children be strong and identify what is theirs in simple language.

Please encourage your child to use the words, "That's mine" to establish ownership over something. You, of course, can add or modify language as needed but be sure it includes the catch phrase, "That's mine." Make sure to use a LOT of praise when they use the catch phrase appropriately, even if prompted!

Here are some ways to practice this skill at home:
• If your child has a sibling, mix up their shoes and/or clothes when helping them get dressed.
• If your child has a sibling, mix up possessions that the children know are their own. Take your child's dessert (or something they really want to eat) and pretend as though you are going to eat it (not in a teasing way but in a 'mistake' manner).
• Pretend you are going to use his/her toothbrush (again, not teasing, but by mistake).

Week 1	Assertiveness Over Ownership of Personal Items
Day 1	Monday — Mix It Up

▪ Introduction to the Topic

"This week, we are going to say, 'That's mine!' when we see our toys from home."

Materials

- Favorite toy from home

Model the Skill

Teacher A picks a toy from a container. Teacher B reaches for the toy and says, "That's mine."

Guided Lesson

1. Children sit in a row on the floor with their toys from home.
2. Each child puts his/her toy in a large container so that the toys are concealed.
3. The teacher picks a toy out of the container and holds it up.
4. If the owner of the toy does not try to reach for it, the teacher shows it to the owner and asks, "Whose toy?"
5. The teacher prompts the owner to take the toy and say, "That's mine."
6. The owner puts the toy back into the container.
7. Repeats steps 3-7 for each child's toy.

* After a few rounds of the teacher picking the toy, children can take on the teacher's role and pick the toy.

Reinforcers

Children are reinforced with verbal praise, physical praise (high fives, tickles, hugs, pats on the back, sensory input), tangibles (stickers), and positive facial expressions for using the words, "That's mine."

Week 1	Assertiveness Over Ownership of Personal Items
Day 2	Tuesday — Scoot to Your Toy

Materials

- Favorite toy from home
- Scooter board

Model the Skill

The teacher models the skill by going down the hallway on a scooter, retrieving a toy, and saying, "That's mine."

Guided Lesson

1. Children sit in a row on the floor (preferably in the hallway).
2. The teacher sits on the opposite end of the hallway with a container holding each child's favorite toy.
3. The teacher picks a toy and asks, "Whose toy?"
4. The owner retrieves his/her toy by using a scooter to get down the hall.
5. When the owner retrieves the toy, he/she says, "That's mine."
6. The owner puts his/her toy back into the container.
7. Repeats steps 3-6 for each child.

Reinforcers

Children are reinforced with verbal praise, physical praise (high fives, tickles, hugs, pats on the back, sensory input), tangibles (stickers), and positive facial expressions for using the words, "That's mine."

Week 1	Assertiveness Over Ownership of Personal Items
Day 3	Wednesday — Run To Your Toy

Materials

- Favorite toy from home

Model the Skill

Teacher A models the skill by running across the room with Teacher B's toy. Teacher B goes across the room and retrieves his/her toy by saying, "That's mine."

Guided Lesson

1. Children sit in a row on the floor.
2. The teacher places toys in front of children, instructing them not to touch the toys.
3. The teacher takes a child's toy and runs across the room with it.
4. The owner goes across the room and retrieves his/her toy by saying, "That's mine."
5. Repeat steps 3-4 with each child.

Reinforcers

Children are reinforced with verbal praise, physical praise (high fives, tickles, hugs, pats on the back, sensory input), tangibles (stickers), and positive facial expressions for using the words, "That's mine."

Week 1 Assertiveness Over Ownership of Personal Items
Day 4   Thursday — Monster Attack

Materials

- Favorite toy from home
- Monster Puppet (named "Momo")

Model the Skill

Teacher A models the skill by using a monster puppet to take Teacher B's toy. Teacher B says, "That's mine." Teacher A returns the toy using the monster puppet.

Guided Lesson

1. Children sit in a row on the floor with their toys.
2. The teacher says, "This is my friend Momo the monster and he is very hungry. He wants to eat your toy."
3. The teacher makes the monster say, "Give me your toy! I want to eat it."
4. The teacher takes a child's toy with the monster puppet.
5. The owner retrieves his/her toy by saying, "That's mine."
6. Repeat steps 3-5 with each child.

Reinforcers

Children are reinforced with verbal praise, physical praise (high fives, tickles, hugs, pats on the back, sensory input), tangibles (stickers), and positive facial expressions for using the words, "That's mine."

Week 1	**Assertiveness Over Ownership of Personal Items**
Day 5	Friday — Slide to Your Toy

Materials

- Favorite toy from home
- Slide structure

Model the Skill

Teacher A models the skill by dropping a toy down the slide to Teacher B. Teacher A goes to Teacher B and retrieves his/her toy by saying, "That's mine." Teacher B returns the toy.

Guided Lesson

1. Children sit in a row on the floor.
2. The teacher picks two children.
3. The teacher places Child A at the top of the slide and Child B at the bottom of the slide.
4. Child A drops his/her toy down the slide to Child B.
5. Child A goes to Child B and retrieves his/her toy by saying, "That's mine." (Do NOT give children their toy unless they use their words!)
6. Child B returns the toy.
7. Have children switch roles.
8. Repeat steps 3-6.
9. Repeat steps 3-6 again with different pairs of children.

Indoor Option

Slide may be substituted with a table. Have children slide their toy across the table. Child A retrieves his/her toy by running around the table to Child B and saying, "That's mine."

Reinforcers

Children are reinforced with verbal praise, physical praise (high fives, tickles, hugs, pats on the back, sensory input), tangibles (stickers), and positive facial expressions for using the words, "That's mine."

Week 1 | Assertiveness Over Ownership of Personal Items
Generalization Ideas For The Classroom

Generalizing "That's Mine!"

- Lunch Box Mix-up: When you pass out the lunch boxes, hand them out to the wrong children or mix them up in their cubbies.

- Clothing/Shoe Mix-up: When the children go outside or at the end of the day, mix up their jackets. If there is any opportunity for them to take off their shoes, mix them up.

- Name Mix-up: If you use written names in circle time or during calendar, give the wrong name to a child.

- Peer Interaction Time: If a child and a peer are engaged with materials, encourage them to verbalize using, "That's mine!" if another child takes something from them.

Books

- Cohen, Miriam. *That's Mine.* Star Bright Books, 2005.
- Sage, Angie, and Chris Sage. *That's Mine, That's Yours.* Penguin, 1991.
- Keller, Holly. *That's Mine, Horace.* Greenwillow Books, 2000.
- Lionni, Leo. *It's Mine!* Dragonfly Books, 1996.

Week 2	**Plays Near Another Child**
	"Playing Near Friends"

Behavioral Objective

Children will learn how to play in close proximity to peers.

Identify the Skill Components

- Onlooking
- Peer awareness

Lessons and Materials for the Week

Day	Lesson	Materials
Monday	Puzzles	Puzzles, mats/carpet squares
Tuesday	Free Play on Mats	Assortment of toys, mats
Wednesday	Free Play in a Play Area	Toys in a play area
Thursday	Favorite Toys at the Table	Favored toys
Friday	Favorite Toys in a Play Area	Favored toys

For the Parents

Dear Parents,

This week, our social skill classroom behavior is:

Category 1: Possessive Understanding/Acknowledgment of Others	
Week 2	Plays Near Another Child "Playing Near Friends"

Many children choose to play in a solitary manner and actively avoid playing near other children. It is critical for their development to begin the process of peer interaction by playing in a "parallel" manner or near other children with similar toys. At this point we are not encouraging interaction, just the act of being near other children.

Please encourage your child to play near or next to other children as much as possible. Most importantly, make sure you identify the skill (e.g., "You are sitting next to that boy!") and use a lot of praise!

Here are some ways to practice this skill at home:
• At the park, take a LOT of sand toys and prompt your child to play next to other children in the sand.
• At the park, prompt your child to pick a swing or climb a structure next to another child.
• If the child has a sibling, have the sibling sit down with toys that the target child enjoys. Give the same toys to the target child and have them sit next to each other and play.
• At the dinner table, have your child choose to sit next to a sibling by name (rather than by the adults).
• At fast food or other casual restaurants, have a child choose to sit at a table that is close to other children.

Week 2	Plays Near Another Child
Day 1	Monday — Puzzles

■ Introduction to the Topic

"This week, we are going to play near our friends."

Materials

- Puzzles
- Mats

Model the Skill

Teacher A builds a puzzle within two feet of Teacher B who is also building a puzzle.

Guided Lesson

1. Place mats on the floor so they are directly next to each other.
2. Place one puzzle in front of each mat on the floor.
3. Have children sit on the mats.
4. Have children do puzzles while sitting next to each other.

Reinforcers

Children are reinforced with verbal praise, physical praise (high fives, tickles, hugs, pats on the back, sensory input), tangibles (stickers), and positive facial expressions for playing near their friends.

| **Week 2** | **Plays Near Another Child** |
| **Day 2** | Tuesday — Free Play on Mats |

Materials

- Assortment of toys
- Mats

Model the Skill

Teacher A and Teacher B sit within two feet of each other and play with the toys directly in front of them.

Guided Lesson

1. Place mats on the floor so they are directly next to each other.
2. Place an assortment of appropriate toys in front of the mats.
3. Have children sit on the mats and tell them that they can pick any toy they like, but they must play while sitting on the mat.
4. Children pick the toys and play while sitting next to each other.

Reinforcers

Children are reinforced with verbal praise, physical praise (high fives, tickles, hugs, pats on the back, sensory input), tangibles (stickers), and positive facial expressions for playing near their friends.

Week 2	**Plays Near Another Child**
Day 3	Wednesday — Free Play in a Play Area

Materials

- Toys in play area

Model the Skill

Teacher A and Teacher B pick toys in the same area and play with their toys in close proximity to each other.

Guided Lesson

1. Bring children to the play area and tell them that they can play with any toy they like, but they must stay in the play area.

2. Help children stay in the play area while playing next to each other.

Reinforcers

Children are reinforced with verbal praise, physical praise (high fives, tickles, hugs, pats on the back, sensory input), tangibles (stickers), and positive facial expressions for playing near their friends.

Week 2   Plays Near Another Child
Day 4   Thursday — Favorite Toys at the Table

Materials

- Favored toys

Model the Skill

Teacher A and Teacher B walk to the table and pick toys to play with next to each other.

Guided Lesson

1. Place favored toys and/or activities (e.g., play dough) on a table.

2. Tell children it is time to play.

3. Children should naturally gravitate to the group table because all of the favored toys/activities are there. Help them sit down if they try to take the toy and leave.

4. If children do not independently go to the table, help guide children there: "Look, the toys are over there!"

Reinforcers

Children are reinforced with verbal praise, physical praise (high fives, tickles, hugs, pats on the back, sensory input), tangibles (stickers), and positive facial expressions for playing near their friends.

Week 2	Plays Near Another Child
Day 5	Friday — Favorite Toys in a Play Area

Materials

- Favored toys

Model the Skill

Teacher A and Teacher B walk to the play area and pick toys to play with next to each other.

Guided Lesson

1. Place favored toys and/or activities (e.g., play dough) in an easy-to-access section of the play area.

2. Tell children it is time to play.

3. Children should naturally gravitate to the play area because all of the favored toys are in plain sight. Help them sit down if they try to take the toy and leave.

4. If children do not independently go to the play area, help guide children there: "Look, the toys are over there!"

Reinforcers

Children are reinforced with verbal praise, physical praise (high fives, tickles, hugs, pats on the back, sensory input), tangibles (stickers), and positive facial expressions for playing near their friends.

Week 2 | Plays Near Another Child
Generalization Ideas For The Classroom

Generalizing "Playing Near Friends"

- Centers: Emphasize curricular centers of 2-3 children this week (if the class is not already designed this way). Allow the first few children to choose their centers on Monday. Encourage the other children to pick a center based on their peer rather than the activity. Ask them to name the peer they will work next to. Throughout the week, alternate which children get to pick first.

Books

- Roffey, Maureen. *Me and My Friends Outdoors*. Discovery Books, 1989.
- Roffey, Maureen. *Me and My Friends Indoors*. Discovery Books, 1989.
- Roffey, Maureen. *Me and My Friends Upstairs*. Discovery Books, 1989.
- Bricknell, Paul. *Baby and Friends*. DK Publishing, 1995.
- Mason, Jane, and Sarah Hines Stephens. *Gymboree Dance Play.* Key Porter Books, 2007.
- Filipek, Nina. *Learning Together: Playing Together*. Illus. Jeannette O'Toole. Autumn Publishing Ltd, 2005.
- Bailey, Debbie. *My Friends*. Annick Press, 2003.

Week 3 | Parallel/Aware Play
"Playing Same"

Behavioral Objective

Children will learn how to onlook to their peers during play and use the information from a peer's play to inform their own play.

Identify the Skill Components

- Onlooking
- Peer awareness

Lessons and Materials for the Week

Day	Lesson	Materials
Monday	Play Dough	Play dough, play dough toys
Tuesday	Musical Instruments	Musical instruments
Wednesday	Cars	Toy cars, car ramp toy (or any ramp)
Thursday	Free Play	Groups of similar toys (instruments, puppets, etc.)
Friday	Follow the Leader	Outdoor equipment (bikes, balls, scooters, etc.), picture cards of outdoor activities

For the Parents

Dear Parents,

This week, our social skill classroom behavior is:

Category 1: Possessive Understanding/Acknowledgment of Others	
Week 3	Parallel/Aware Play "Playing Same"

Many children may play near another child, but are so focused on their own interests that they do not expand their skills by learning from others. They may be next to other children but no modeling or copying of behavior occurs. Imitation is critical for learning in both academics and social situations.

Please encourage your child to play near other children and copy what they do. Make sure to identify and praise your child for being near a peer and imitating them: "You are sitting with that boy and both of you are pouring sand! That's amazing!"

Here are some ways to practice this skill at home:
• At the park, use the sand toys and sit with your child as they sit with another child. Point to what the other child is doing and prompt your child to copy him/her as you do the same. Most typical children are happy if someone attends to them and thinks what they are doing is "cool."
• At the park, as your child is on a swing next to another child, prompt him/her to make the same facial expressions or verbalizations as the other child.
• At the park, ask another child to be the "leader" and model how to use the playground structures. Have your child follow and imitate the peer's play.
• If your child has a sibling, give both children the same toys or materials and encourage the sibling to model various activities. If an older or younger sibling is available, they should be utilized as often as possible; lots of copycat!
• At the dinner table, have everyone copy one person (hopefully a sibling or another child if possible). Have that person eat food in a particular order or silly way.

Week 3 Parallel/Aware Play
Day 1 Monday — Play Dough

■ Introduction to the Topic

"This week, we are going to play the same as our friends."

Materials

- Play dough
- Play dough toys

Model the Skill

Teacher A plays with the play dough and a toy, and then passes them to Teacher B. It is important for Teacher B to exaggerate his/her onlooking (e.g., with wide eyes or a craned neck). Teacher B should be watching what Teacher A does intently. Teacher B plays with the play dough in the same manner as Teacher A.

Guided Lesson

1. Sit children around a table.
2. Give one child play dough and a toy.
3. Have other children watch what the child is doing for a few seconds.
4. Pass the play dough to the next child and have the child do the same action on the play dough with the same toy.

Reinforcers

Children are reinforced with verbal praise, physical praise (high fives, tickles, hugs, pats on the back, sensory input), tangibles (stickers), and positive facial expressions for doing the same thing as their friends.

Week 3	Parallel/Aware Play
Day 2	Tuesday — Musical Instruments

Materials

- Musical instruments

Model the Skill

Teacher A plays a musical instrument and then passes it to Teacher B. Teacher B plays the same instrument as Teacher A.

Guided Lesson

1. Have children sit on the floor in a circle.

2. Give one child a musical instrument (e.g., xylophone, drum, bells, tambourine, maracas). Any action by the child is acceptable (even if the child does something silly or incorrect). If the child needs help engaging with the instrument, use hand-over-hand to make a movement or sound with the instrument.

3. Have other children watch what the child is doing for a few seconds.

4. Pass the musical instrument to the next child, and have the child play the instrument in the same manner.

Reinforcers

Children are reinforced with verbal praise, physical praise (high fives, tickles, hugs, pats on the back, sensory input), tangibles (stickers), and positive facial expressions for making music just like their friends.

Week 3	Parallel/Aware Play
Day 3	Wednesday — Cars

Materials

- Cars: two to three per child (each car should identically match a car held by another child)
- Car ramp toys (or any ramps)

Model the Skill

Teacher A rolls a car down a ramp. Teacher A should label the car something fun (e.g., "downtown brown"), and send it down the ramp with a certain style, sound, or pressure. Teacher A can verbalize the particular style by saying, "I'm pushing downtown brown hard down the blue ramp (with 'zoom' sound)." Teacher B watches and then performs the same action with an identical "downtown brown" car.

Guided Lesson

1. Set the car ramps on a table.
2. Tell the children "We are going to play with cars today."
3. Tell the children, "All of these cars have names and have ways they like to drive. Some of them are the same. You can push them fast or slow, hard or soft; you can pick a ramp, and you can make a sound (demonstrate each). When it's your turn, you can pick the way you like your car to drive and your friends will watch and copy you."
4. Pick the first child and have him/her select a car and name it, if possible. If not, a teacher can name it. The child shows his/her peers how the car likes to drive. The teacher then finds the child with the identical car and encourages him/her to drive it in the same manner.
5. Encourage children to look at what their peers are doing.
6. Have a brief free time play and encourage the children to watch each other and copy their peers' style. Even if it's with different cars, the focus is on watching the peer.

Reinforcers

Children are reinforced with verbal praise, physical praise (high fives, tickles, hugs, pats on the back, sensory input), tangibles (stickers), and positive facial expressions for doing the same thing as their friends.

Week 3	**Parallel/Aware Play**
Day 4	Thursday — Free Play

Materials

- Groups of similar toys in various categories (musical instruments, puppets, etc.)

Model the Skill

Teacher A picks a toy and plays with it. Teacher B picks a toy from the same group and plays with it.

Guided Lesson

1. Sit children at a table.

2. Give one child a choice between two toys.

3. Have other children watch what the child is choosing to play with.

4. Give the other children two options in toys as well, but instruct them to "pick same."

5. Prompt the children to pick the same type of toy as the first child.

Reinforcers

Children are reinforced with verbal praise, physical praise (high fives, tickles, hugs, pats on the back, sensory input), tangibles (stickers), and positive facial expressions for doing the same thing as their friends.

Week 3	**Parallel/Aware Play**
Day 5	Friday — Follow the Leader

Materials

- Outdoor equipment (bikes, balls, scooter boards)
- Picture cards of outdoor activities that include equipment you have available (can be from calendars, magazines, or speech and language action cards)

Model the Skill

Teacher A picks a picture of an outdoor activity then imitates the activity. Teacher B follows Teacher A and does the same activity.

Guided Lesson

1. Sit children together outside.
2. Nominate one child to be the "leader" and pick what the group will play.
3. Give them options using real-life pictures (e.g., riding bikes, playing with balls or scooter boards).
4. Have the "leader" pick an activity from the picture cards.
5. Help the other children complete the "leader's" choice of activity.
6. Repeat steps 2-5 with all the other children in the group, giving everyone a chance to be the "leader."

Indoor Option

Outdoor equipment may be substituted with indoor toys such as puzzles, dollhouse toys, pretend food and blocks. For example, all children pretend to eat food.

Reinforcers

Children are reinforced with verbal praise, physical praise (high fives, tickles, hugs, pats on the back, sensory input), tangibles (stickers), and positive facial expressions for doing the same thing as their friends.

Week 3 | Parallel/Aware Play
Generalization Ideas For The Classroom

Generalizing "Playing Same"

- Centers: Building upon the theme of "Playing Near Friends" from Week 2, emphasize curricular centers of 2-3 children. Have the first child carry out an activity while his/her peers engage in similar modeling. Again, encourage the other children to pick a center based on their peer rather than the activity. Ask them to name the peer they will work next to and encourage them to copy their peer's work. Throughout the week, alternate which children get to pick first. Clearly, the teacher must pick centers where copying other children is appropriate (e.g., a letter activity where they are putting on decorations; maybe one child decorates using beans and that becomes the model).

Books

- Ritchey, Kate, ed. *Can You? Waddle Like a Penguin?* Price Stern Sloan, 2006.

- Silverman, Erica. *Follow the Leader.* Farrar Straus Giroux, 2000.

- Clark, Emma Chichester. *Follow the Leader!* Margaret K. McElderry Books, 2003.

- Boynton, Sandra. *But Not the Hippopotamus.* Little Simon, 1982.

- Carley, Lorina B. *Clap Your Hands Board Book.* Putnam Juvenile, 1997.

- Edwards, Richard. *Copy Me CopyCub.* Scholastic, 2001.

- Inkpen, Mick. *If I Had a Pig.* MacMillan Kids, 2000.

- Inkpen, Mick. *If I Had a Sheep.* Yearling, 1992.

Week 4 | Interacts with Other Children
"Talking to Friends"

Behavioral Objective

Children will learn the basics of peer interaction skills and carry them out.

NOTE:

This unit is best for two children at a time.

Identify the Skill Components

- Language
- Ability to maintain eye contact (at least briefly)
- Ability to maintain attention for a specified amount of time
- Peer awareness

Lessons and Materials for the Week

Day	Lesson	Materials
Monday	Ball Roll	Ball
Tuesday	Cut and Paste	Scissors, paper, glue
Wednesday	Hot Potato	CD Player, ball/stuffed animal or other soft item to pass
Thursday	Ball Patterns	Small Ball
Friday	Instruments	Instruments

For the Parents

Dear Parents,

This week, our social skill classroom behavior is:

Category 1: Possessive Understanding/Acknowledgment of Others	
Week 4	Interacts with Other Children "Talking to Friends"

Many children use language but have not directed it towards other children, nor utilized it to initiate interaction. We begin to develop these skills by providing very structured and clear situations to allow a child to feel safe to initiate interaction with other children.

Please encourage your child to address other children and siblings by name during interactions, using the basic phrase, "Here____." If neither are present, you can practice with your child directly. Make sure to identify and praise your child for utilizing the phrase, "Here____," especially when expressed spontaneously.

Here are some ways to practice this skill at home:
• With a sibling or another child, have your child participate in a cleaning or washing activity by passing a sponge and taking turns saying, "Here____."
• Have your child be the dinner server and hand out plates, utensils, and food, using the phrase, "Here ____," particularly with siblings or peers.
• In the bathtub, play sponge-toss or squeeze-toy-toss with siblings using the phrase, "Here____."
• In the car, if a sibling or peer asks for something, pass the item to the target child first so that he/she can hand it to the sibling/peer saying, "Here ____."
• In any situation, have your child be the "messenger" by delivering things to others (particularly siblings) using the phrase, "Here____."

Week 4 Interacts with Other Children
Day 1 Monday — Ball Roll

■ **Introduction to the Topic**

"This week, we are learning about talking to our friends."

Materials

- Ball

Model the Skill

Teacher A rolls the ball to Teacher B and says, "Here (teacher's name)."

Guided Lesson

1. Children sit across from each other, about 5-6 feet apart, with their legs spread out.
2. Each child takes turns rolling or bouncing the ball to a peer.
3. Children are prompted to say, "Here _____" before they roll.

Reinforcers

Children are reinforced with verbal praise, physical praise (high fives, tickles, hugs, pats on the back, sensory input), tangibles (stickers), and positive facial expressions for talking to their friends.

Week 4	**Interacts with Other Children**
Day 2	Tuesday — Cut and Paste

Materials

- Scissors
- Paper
- Glue

Model the Skill

Teacher A cuts shapes and hands them to Teacher B saying, "Here____."
Teacher B glues them on to a piece of paper.

Guided Lesson

1. Children work together in pairs to create a shape picture.
2. One child cuts all the shapes and hands them to the other child.
3. Children are prompted to say, "Here _____," when they pass their shape.
4. This child, in turn, glues all the shapes onto a blank piece of paper.

Reinforcers

Children are reinforced with verbal praise, physical praise (high fives, tickles, hugs, pats on the back, sensory input), tangibles (stickers), and positive facial expressions for talking to their friends.

Week 4 Interacts with Other Children
Day 3 Wednesday — Hot Potato

Materials

- CD player
- Ball, stuffed animal, or other soft item to pass

Model the Skill

With music playing, Teacher A passes a soft item to Teacher B, then Teacher B passes it back, and so on. Each time, the teachers say, "Here ____," making sure to address the other by name. When the music stops, everyone freezes.

Guided Lesson

1. Children sit across from each other, about 5-6 feet apart.
2. Teachers assist each child in passing an item to a peer.
3. Children are prompted to say, "Here _____," before they pass.
4. When the music stops, help the child who has the item freeze. The other children can freeze as well but it is not a focus of the lesson. The teachers can then cheer.

Reinforcers

Children are reinforced with verbal praise, physical praise (high fives, tickles, hugs, pats on the back, sensory input), tangibles (stickers), and positive facial expressions for talking to their friends.

Week 4	Interacts with Other Children
Day 4	Thursday — Ball Patterns

Materials

- Small ball

Model the Skill

Teacher A demonstrates a pattern with the small ball (e.g., placing the ball on his/her head, shoulder, knee). Teacher A passes the ball to Teacher B and says, "Here_____." Teacher B imitates the same pattern.

Guided Lesson

1. Children sit across from each other on the floor.
2. The teacher gives each child in the pair a small ball.
3. Child A demonstrates a simple 2- or 3-step pattern with the ball.
4. Child A passes the ball to Child B, saying, "Here _____."
5. Child B imitates the pattern.
6. The children switch roles.

Reinforcers

Children are reinforced with verbal praise, physical praise (high fives, tickles, hugs, pats on the back, sensory input), tangibles (stickers), and positive facial expressions for imitating and talking to their friends.

Week 4	**Interacts with Other Children**
Day 5	Friday — Instruments

Materials

- Instruments

Model the Skill

Teacher A plays an instrument and passes it to Teacher B saying, "Here_____."
Teacher B plays the instrument in the same manner.

Guided Lesson

1. Children sit in a circle on the floor.

2. One child picks an instrument and plays it.

3. Children receive the instrument, play it a little, and then pass it around saying, "Here_____."

4. If a child plays the instrument in the same manner as a previous child, he/she can be praised for watching his/her friends.

Reinforcers

Children are reinforced with verbal praise, physical praise (high fives, tickles, hugs, pats on the back, sensory input), tangibles (stickers), and positive facial expressions for talking to their friends.

Week 4 | Interacts with Other Children
Generalization Ideas For The Classroom

Generalizing "Talking to Friends"

- Have children pass items out to one another and address each other by name, saying, "Here_____." Possible items include papers, materials, lunches, utensils and plates.

- When children line up to transition, give the first child a fun object to look at (e.g., squishy ball, rain stick) and have them pass it down the line using the catch phrase, "Here_____."

- Play outdoor games that might include passing balls, beanbags, or even bikes/scooters using the catch phrase, "Here_____."

- Have children wash the tables after activities (eating, art) and give them 10 swirls with the sponge. Have them pass it to a friend saying the catch phrase, "Here_____."

- If children participate in a calendar activity, every time they come to the board to place something, give the item to another child and have him/her hand it to the target child using, "Here_____." Vary this to give all students an opportunity to hand something to a peer.

- Establish a leader for a particular activity and have him/her pass out snacks or supplies using the catch phrase, "Here_____."

Books

- Baker, Sue, and Annie Kubler. *Pass the Parcel.* Child's Play, Int'l, 2005.

- Banks, Jane Whelen. *Liam Says "Hi": Learning to Greet a Friend.* Jessica Kingsley Publishers, 2008.

- Hall, Kirsten. *Duck, Duck, Goose! (My First Reader).* Illus. Laura Rader. Children's Press, 2004.

- Kitamura, Satoshi. *Play With Me! (Dottie Duck).* Farrar, Straus and Giroux, 1996.

- Powell, Richard, and Stuart Trotter. *Play With Me! (Peep-O-Book).* Treehouse Children's Books Ltd, 1997.

- Ross, Michael Elsohn. *Play with Me.* Illus. Julie Downing. Tricycle Press, 2009.

- Donovan, Mary Lee, and Cynthia Jabar. *Won't You Come and Play with Me?* Houghton Mifflin Books for Children, 1998.

Week 5	Expressive Ownership: Refuse/Retrieve Belongings
	"Can I Have It Back Please?"

Behavioral Objective

Children will learn to retrieve their personal belongings using polite and appropriate language.

NOTE:

This week's curriculum is an expansion of Week 1 "Assertiveness Over Ownership of Personal Items." Also note that toys or possessions must be brought from home and belong to the child; they cannot be a part of the collective classroom.

Identify the Skill Components

- Recognition of a favorite toy as their own
- Language: verbalizing. The child should be able to say, at a minimum, "Can I have a turn please?"
- Ability to retrieve belongings
- Ability to care for personal belongings and ideas
- Ability to pass and accept items from peers
- Ability to regulate and control impulses

Lessons and Materials for the Week

Day	Lesson	Materials
Monday	Hide and Seek	Clear plastic bags, personal toys from home
Tuesday	Flubber	Moon sand, sand toys that form shapes from home, flubber, cookie cutters from home, paper
Wednesday	Unfinished Drawings	Report folders, crayons/markers, teacher-created drawing starters
Thursday	Reverse "Go Fish"	Kids set of "Go Fish" cards
Friday	Modified Apples to Apples®	Category picture cards (from flashcard sets, other games, or magazines), specific item cards (fruits, vegetables, colors, etc.)

NOTE:

Monday and Tuesday's lessons involve the child's personal possessions from home. Be sure to ask parents to bring in the materials listed above in advance.

For the Parents

Dear Parents,

This week, our social skill classroom behavior is:

Category 1: Possessive Understanding/Acknowledgment of Others	
Week 5	Expressive Ownership Refuse/Retrieve Belongings "Can I Have It Back Please?"

Many children do not assert themselves when something belongs to them and is taken away. It is important for us to help children be strong and identify what is theirs. Furthermore, it is important for them to do this in a polite and appropriate way. It is imperative for them to understand that they can have their things but that it is polite to eventually share and to use appropriate language.

Please encourage your child to use the catch phrase "That's mine!" to establish ownership over his/her belongings. Encourage your child to ask for an item back and acknowledge that it can be used later using the following phrases:

"That's mine. Can I have it back please?"
"You can use it later."
"You can have a turn after me."

Make sure to use a LOT of praise when they use the above catch phrases appropriately (even if prompted).

Here are some ways to practice this skill at home:
• Bring loads of sand toys to the park and leave them in a particular area. When other children come to use the toys, facilitate appropriate language in your child (be polite, allow others to use it later, etc.).
• As in Week 1, if your child has a sibling, mix up their shoes, socks and other possessions when giving them things to facilitate appropriate language.
• Take an item from your child (not in a teasing manner but as a "mistake") and encourage him/her to ask for it back politely and, if appropriate, allow you a turn later.
• At any point during a play date, observe and take advantage of any opportunity to generalize the skill, "That's mine. Can I have it back please?"

Week 5	Expressive Ownership: Refuse/Retrieve Belongings
Day 1	Monday — Hide and Seek

▪ Introduction to the Topic

"Remember when we played those games with our favorite toys a while ago? We have our favorite toys here again this week. Today, we are going to practice letting all the kids know that your toy belongs to you, using polite and nice words. Our toys are going to hide from us today and each one of you will get a turn to find all the toys and give them back to their owners!"

Materials

- Plastic grocery or clear bags
- Personal toys from home

Model the Skill

Teacher A puts a toy in a plastic bag and states, "This is my toy in a bag. It's different from our classroom toys because I brought it from home and it's in the bag." Teacher A then tells Teacher B to close his/her eyes while Teacher A models hiding the toy. Teacher B goes to find the toy and then holds it up. Teacher A says, "You found my toy! Can I have it back please?"

Guided Lesson

1. Children sit on the floor in a line against a wall on one side of the room.

2. Children put their toys in a plastic bag. The reason for this is so that the seeking child knows that the "bagged" toys are the items to be found and not just toys in the classroom; it distinguishes the children's home toys from the classroom materials.

3. The teacher picks one target child to stay seated, turn and face the wall, and close his/her eyes. This child keeps his/her own toy in a bag to the side.

4. The other children go and hide their toys in the room.

5. When they are finished, they come back to the wall and sit down.

6. The target child then goes around the room to find all the kids' toys.

7. Children are free to cheer, use "hot/cold," and give clues in a fun and playful manner.

8. When the target child finds a toy, all the teachers and children cheer, and the child to whom the toy belongs uses the catch phrase, "You found my toy! Can I have it back please?"

9. Repeat the activity, giving all the children a turn to "seek."

Reinforcers

Use "thank you" along with lots of cheering and verbal praise, and allow the children a few minutes to play with their toys.

Week 5	**Expressive Ownership: Refuse/Retrieve Belongings**
Day 2	Tuesday — Flubber

Materials

- Moon sand
- Sand toys from home (ones that form: cups, moon sand shapers, castle shapes)
- Flubber
- Cookie cutters from home
- Two 8 ½" x 11" cards, a set for each table: one with a happy face and a child giving (representing "It's mine, but you can have a turn"), and one with a neutral face and a clock (representing "Sorry, not now but later.")

Model the Skill

The teacher describes the cards and tells the children they can choose whichever response they want if someone requests their cookie cutters. Teacher A models how to request, "Can I have a turn with your cutter?" and Teacher B responds by holding up one of the signs and saying, "Sorry, not now but later," or "It's mine, but you can have a turn." Teachers emphasize that if they say, "Sorry, not now but later," they will have to share the item the next time. The signs are only needed to facilitate prompting. If the children just need verbal prompts, the teacher can cue the child verbally (e.g., "Sorry___," or "It's___").

Guided Lesson

1. Children sit together at a table.
2. Children are asked to show what items they brought.
3. The teacher splits the children into groups: half at the sand area with the sand toys, and half at the flubber area with the cookie cutters.
4. The teacher waits for children to spontaneously request the items they want from their peers.
5. If time goes by and interaction does not occur, the teacher should use attractive language to get children to request (e.g., "Wow, look at that great shape Johnny made. Maybe you can make one of those?").

Reinforcers

Reinforcement occurs naturally in that the child is getting the item they are requesting. Teachers use verbal praise, physical praise (high fives, tickles, hugs, pats on the back, sensory input), tangibles (stickers), and positive facial expressions to reinforce appropriate behavior.

Week 5	**Expressive Ownership: Refuse/Retrieve Belongings**
Day 3	Wednesday — Unfinished Drawings

Materials

- Report folders
- Crayons/markers/colored pencils
- Teacher-created drawing starters on 8 ½" x 11" paper. The number required depends on the number of children; if you have eight children, you need to create eight frames and photocopy a booklet for each child. The eight frames should just be creative black outline drawings such as:

  a. A few children running on the left side of the paper with a caption at the top that says, "We're running from the scary_____," and a big, blank space on the right side of the paper. Children can come up with something to draw in the blank space that is chasing the children.

  b. A kangaroo with a line for an empty pouch and a caption that says, "Wait, this is not my baby kangaroo!" Children can come up with something other than a kangaroo baby to go in the pouch.

  c. A child sitting on a dock with a fishing rod with nothing on it and a caption that says, "Look what I caught!" Children can come up with a creature or object that could be caught by a fisherman.

Model the Skill

The teacher has the children sit at a round or kidney-shaped table so they can all see each other. Crayons/markers/pencils are given to the children. Teacher holds up a picture and says, "We are going to finish my drawings and create a book. I'm going to give each of you the same copy of my drawings and we are going to come up with ideas that we can all use and share with each other."

Guided Lesson

1. Children sit at a table where they can all see each other.
2. The teacher hands out the first frame (such as the fishing rod line drawing).
3. The teacher says, "This is a picture of a boy fishing and this writing says, 'Look what I caught!' Before you draw on your page, please raise your hand and share if you have an idea of something he can catch." Many children with developmental disabilities have a hard time creating ideas so if none of the children have a suggestion, a second teacher can prompt by whispering an appropriate idea for a child to share. The teacher says, "That's a GREAT idea, we should all have the boy catch a ____." As the

other children start to copy, the child who came up with the scenario is prompted to say, "That was my idea but you can all use it too!"

4. Manipulate the situation to ensure that each child has one opportunity to share an idea and use the catch phrase, "That was my idea but you can all use it too!"

5. At the end, have the children put their completed drawings into the report folders.

6. The teacher should conclude by going through the folder page by page and praising each idea. The children should be prompted to point and say, "That one was my idea!"

Reinforcers

Ensure that all the children are praising each other for coming up with good ideas. Hang the artwork on the wall and have the children go around to other staff and parents identifying which idea was theirs using the catch phrase, "That one was my idea!"

Week 5	**Expressive Ownership: Refuse/Retrieve Belongings**
Day 4	Thursday — Reverse "Go Fish"

Materials

- Kids set of "Go Fish" cards

Model the Skill

Teacher A takes five cards and Teacher B takes five cards (make sure to arrange the cards so that the first 3-4 cards at the top of the turned-down deck are matches to the cards held by the teachers). Teacher A draws a card and asks Teacher B if he/she has a match. Teacher B responds, "Yes, thank you!" Teacher A gives Teacher B the card. Repeat the model a few more times.

Guided Lesson

1. The teacher explains, "We're going to play a game where you want to give your friends matches of their cards!"

2. The teacher hands out five cards to each child.

3. Children are instructed to put any matches from the dealt hand down in front of them.

4. The first child draws a card and looks at it. If there is no match, he/she picks another child and tries to give that card to a peer. If the child has a match, he/she says, "Thank you." If the child does not have a match, he/she says, "Thank you, but I don't need that now." The first child keeps the card if no match is found.

5. If children want to keep score, keep track of how many times they give a card to another child.

Reinforcers

Praise and group congratulations for helping other children.

Week 5	Expressive Ownership: Refuse/Retrieve Belongings
Day 5	Friday — Modified Apples to Apples®

Materials

- Category pictures: You can use magazine cut-outs pasted on cards, language cards, or any cards from various games. Categories can include fruits, vegetables, colors, vehicles, ice cream flavors, and candy

Model the Skill

Teacher says, "We're going to try and guess other people's favorite things! Look, you all have pictures of different fruits in your hand. Put down the one you think is my favorite." Children choose a card from their hands and the teacher shows them how to place it facedown on the table. The teacher then models flipping over the cards, labeling them, and identifying his/her favorite. "Oh! A peach, a plum, an apple and a pear. My favorite is the apple! Who thought it was an apple?"

Guided Lesson

1. Teacher deals out all of the cards in one category to everyone except one child. Kids should have two or three cards to choose from.
2. The child with no cards says, "Pick my favorite___" (e.g., color).
3. Each child picks a card and puts it in the middle of the table face down.
4. When all the children have chosen a card, the child with no cards mixes them up, turns them all over, and picks the one that is his/her favorite.
5. Children are encouraged to yell out, "That was my card!" if their card was picked.
6. Repeat so each child has a turn with each category (every child does ice cream flavors, every child does fruit, etc.).
7. If the teacher wants to add a competitive aspect to it, every time a child's card gets picked and he/she says, "That was my card," he/she gets a token (a stone, marble, sticker, star, etc.). By the end of the game, the child who has the most tokens wins. This means a child wins because he/she is able to think about what other children like most effectively.

NOTE:

It is possible that children will forget which card they chose as their idea for the other child's favorite. Part of this game is also developing recall skills. The teacher can modify the game a bit if children are having difficulty recalling by allowing them to leave their card face down in front of them. If they can remember their selections, however, mixing it up is better.

Reinforcers

Praise children for remembering other children's favorite things. Also, teachers can include a "favorite flavor" of a particular candy (e.g. watermelon, grape, strawberry, lemon) in the guided practice and include that candy at the end. Have the group try to remember other children's favorite flavors and hand out flavors for fun.

Week 5 | Expressive Ownership: Refuse/Retrieve Belongings
Generalization Ideas For The Classroom

Generalizing "Can I Have It Back Please?"

- Have children bring in equipment from home for outside playtime and practice using the language, "It's mine, but you can have a turn," and "That's my toy. Can I have it back please?"

- Similar to Week 1, mix up lunch boxes, clothing, shoes, or names and encourage statements building from, "That's mine (my lunchbox, my purple sweatshirt). Can I have it back please?"

- Leave toys and materials that belong to the children in the classroom for free use after the structured activities earlier in the week (note that the last three days of activities are not "toy-based"). Children can continue to identify their toys, use polite refusal language, or use sharing language (e.g., "It's mine but you can have a turn" or "Sorry, not now but later").

Books

- Verdick, Elizabeth. *Sharing Time (Toddler Tools)*. Illus. Marieka Heinlen. Free Spirit Publishing, 2009.

- Berry, Joy. *Let's Talk About Saying "NO"*. Scholastic Inc., 1996.

- Huang, Benrei. *Hey, That's Mine!: A Child's Book about Sharing*. Standard Publishing Company, 1997.

- Wheeler, Valerie. *Yes, Please! No, Thank You!* Illus. Glin Dibley. Sterling, 2006.

- Stuart, Carole. *The Thank You Book*. Illus. Arthur Robins. Running Press, 2003.

Week 6	**Shows Displeasure Verbally Instead of Physically**
	"Awww Man!"

Behavioral Objective

Children will learn to express displeasure verbally and to control negative emotions.

Identify the Skill Components

- Language
- Ability to comprehend displeasure
- Ability to identify displeasure in peers
- Ability to control negative emotions

Lessons and Materials for the Week

Day	Lesson	Materials
Monday	Jenga®	Jenga® board game
Tuesday	Chutes and Ladders®	Chutes and Ladders® board game
Wednesday	Operation®	Operation® board game
Thursday	Dominoes	Domino pieces
Friday	Don't Break the Ice®	Don't Break the Ice® board game

For the Parents

Dear Parents,

This week, our social skill classroom behavior is:

Category 1: Possessive Understanding/Acknowledgment of Others	
Week 6	Shows Displeasure Verbally Instead of Physically "Awww Man!"

It is critically important for children to learn to express displeasure verbally and control negative emotions. In a classroom situation, at a birthday party, at a play date, or at the park, children must not throw a tantrum, aggress towards others, or get up and leave because they have lost or are disappointed about something. This week, we are encouraging your child to say, "Awww man!" instead of getting truly upset, agitated or physical.

Here are some ways to practice this skill at home:
- Use any board game that does not allow your child to win automatically. The ones we're using in class that can be repeated at home are: Don't Break the Ice®, Jenga®, Chutes and Ladders®, and Operation®.
- Before the game begins, remind your child to say, "Awww man!" when they don't get what they want or expect. Games that offer many turns and equal chances of success/failure are good to use such as Cranium Cadoo®, Lucky Ducks®, Old MacDonald Had a Farm™, and Barnyard Bingo™.
- It's great to practice throughout a game rather than just when it's over, so choose games accordingly.
- Use excessive praise when a child responds appropriately!

Week 6 | Shows Displeasure Verbally Instead of Physically
Day 1 | Monday — Jenga®

■ **Introduction to the Topic**

"This week, we are going to learn how to use our words when we don't win. When we don't win or things don't go our way, we can say, 'Awww man!'"

Materials

- Jenga® board game

Model the Skill

Teacher A models the skill by saying, "Awww man!" when the Jenga® tower falls.

Guided Lesson

1. Children sit in a circle at the table.

2. Children take turns taking one block off the Jenga® tower and placing it on top of the tower.

3. Children are prompted to say, "Awww man!" when the tower falls.

Reinforcers

Children are reinforced with verbal praise, physical praise (high fives, tickles, hugs, pats on the back, sensory input), tangibles (stickers), and positive facial expressions for expressing displeasure verbally.

Week 6 Shows Displeasure Verbally Instead of Physically
Day 2   Tuesday — Chutes and Ladders®

Materials

- Chutes and Ladders® board game

Model the Skill

Teacher A models the skill by saying, "Awww man!" when he/she falls down the slide.

Guided Lesson

1. Children sit in a circle at the table.
2. Children take turns moving their players forward.
3. Children are prompted to say, "Awww man!" when their player falls down the slide.

Reinforcers

Children are reinforced with verbal praise, physical praise (high fives, tickles, hugs, pats on the back, sensory input), tangibles (stickers), and positive facial expressions for expressing displeasure verbally.

Week 6	**Shows Displeasure Verbally Instead of Physically**
Day 3	Wednesday — Operation®

Materials

- Operation® board game

Model the Skill

Teacher A models the skill by saying, "Awww man!" when the buzzer rings.

Guided Lesson

1. Children sit in a circle at the table.
2. Children take turns removing body parts from the operation board.
3. Children are prompted to say, "Awww man!" when the buzzer rings.

Reinforcers

Children are reinforced with verbal praise, physical praise (high fives, tickles, hugs, pats on the back, sensory input), tangibles (stickers), and positive facial expressions for expressing displeasure verbally.

Week 6	Shows Displeasure Verbally Instead of Physically
Day 4	Thursday — Dominoes

Materials

- Domino Pieces

Model the Skill

Teacher A models the skill by lining up the dominoes and saying, "Awww man!" when the domino pieces fall.

Guided Lesson

1. Children sit in a circle at the table.
2. Children take turns lining up the domino pieces.
3. Children are prompted to say, "Awww man!" when the domino pieces fall.

Reinforcers

Children are reinforced with verbal praise, physical praise (high fives, tickles, hugs, pats on the back, sensory input), tangibles (stickers), and positive facial expressions for expressing displeasure verbally.

Week 6	Shows Displeasure Verbally Instead of Physically
Day 5	Friday — Don't Break the Ice®

Materials

- Don't Break the Ice® board game

Model the Skill

Teacher A models the skill by saying, "Awww man!" when the ice breaks.

Guided Lesson

1. Children sit in a circle at the table.
2. Children take turns hitting the ice pieces off.
3. Children are prompted to say, "Awww man!" when the ice plate breaks.

Reinforcers

Children are reinforced with verbal praise, physical praise (high fives, tickles, hugs, pats on the back, sensory input), tangibles (stickers), and positive facial expressions for expressing displeasure verbally.

Week 6 Shows Displeasure Verbally Instead of Physically
Generalization Ideas For The Classroom

Generalizing "Awww Man!"

- Any game that includes opportunities for frequent successes/failures can be put out for children to play during free time (e.g., Cranium Cadoo®, Barnyard Bingo™, Lucky Ducks®, Old MacDonald Had a Farm™). Supervise loosely, encourage, and praise appropriate language.

- Start a system this week that uses colored beads during lineup. Give out all black beads with the exception of one blue bead. If a child gets the blue bead, he/she is the line leader. Encourage the children who get the black beads to say, "Awww man!" You can utilize this same system in other leadership situations (e.g., snack helper).

- During calendar, you can incorporate "Awww man!" if a child doesn't get quite what he/she expects (e.g., a turn).

Books

- Malam, John. *My First Mr. Bump Book.* Illus. Adam Hargreaves. Egmont Books Ltd, 1997.

- Banks, Jane Whelen. *Liam Wins the Game, Sometimes: A Story About Losing With Grace.* Jessica Kingsley Pub, 2008.

- Parker, David. *I Can Be Fair.* Illus. Meredith Johnson. Scholastic, 2005.

Week 7 | Asserts Self in Socially Appropriate Ways
"Be Strong"

Behavioral Objective

Children will learn to assert themselves in socially appropriate ways.

Identify the Skill Components

- Language
- Ability to make decisions
- Ability to follow directions from a peer
- Ability to use appropriate gestures

Lessons and Materials for the Week

Day	Lesson	Materials
Monday	Simon Says	None
Tuesday	Child as Leader	Don't Break the Ice® board game
Wednesday	Child as Chooser	Duck, Duck Goose® board game, Lucky Ducks® board game
Thursday	Obstacle Course	Slide, bikes, chalk
Friday	Pointing/Word Game	Three toys that possess different characteristics, three chairs

For the Parents

Dear Parents,

This week, our social skill classroom behavior is:

Category 1: Possessive Understanding/Acknowledgment of Others	
Week 7	Asserts Self in Socially Appropriate Ways "Be Strong"

It is critically important for children to learn how to use a strong body and voice when speaking to others. This means they cannot hide behind your legs, look down, look to the side, or speak in a quiet voice. When addressing others, children must "be strong."

Please encourage your children to "be strong." Any time you take your children into the community, preempt and prompt them to "be strong" when they speak to others (the grocery store clerk, the mailman, the waitress). You can prompt them with the language to reduce the pressure but ensure they speak in a strong voice, face the person, and maintain eye contact.

Here are some ways to practice this skill at home:
• Have your child direct a task using a toy microphone to indicate that he/she is in charge. For example, at bath time, your child can pretend to be a captain and tell you what body parts to help wash.
• When you play physical games with your child, encourage the use of strong words such as, "Get off!"
• Use excessive praise when a child responds appropriately! If your child uses words in a strong manner, even if he/she cannot have the desired item, praise him/her for "being strong."

Week 7	**Asserts Self in Socially Appropriate Ways**
Day 1	Monday — Simon Says *(Emphasis: Being strong with your words)*

■ Introduction to the Topic

"This week, we are learning about 'being strong.' Our bodies, our eyes, our faces, and our voices need to show everyone that WE ARE STRONG AND SMART!"

Materials

- None

Model the Skill

The teacher models the skill by being "Simon." The teacher uses an assertive voice to tell children to touch different parts of their bodies.

Guided Lesson

1. Children sit in a row on the floor.
2. Children take turns being "Simon."
3. When a child is "Simon," he/she must use a strong (i.e., loud) voice to tell the other children to touch different parts of their bodies.
4. Repeat so that each child has the opportunity to be "Simon."

Reinforcers

Children are reinforced with verbal praise, physical praise (high fives, tickles, hugs, pats on the back, sensory input), tangibles (stickers), and positive facial expressions for doing a great job being strong with their words.

Week 7 | Asserts Self in Socially Appropriate Ways
Day 2 | Tuesday — Child as Leader *(Emphasis: Being strong with your words)*

Materials

- Don't Break the Ice® board game

Model the Skill

The teacher models the skill by using an assertive voice and telling children who goes first, how many pieces of ice to break, and who goes next.

Guided Lesson

1. Children sit in a circle on the floor.
2. The teacher picks one child to be the leader.
3. The leader uses a strong voice to lead the game.
4. The leader tells his/her peers who goes first.
5. The leader tells his/her peers how many pieces of ice to break.
6. The leader tells his/her peers who goes next.
7. Repeat so that all children have the chance to be the leader.

Reinforcers

Children are reinforced with verbal praise, physical praise (high fives, tickles, hugs, pats on the back, sensory input), tangibles (stickers), and positive facial expressions for doing a great job being strong with their words.

Week 7 Asserts Self in Socially Appropriate Ways
Day 3 Wednesday — Child as Chooser *(Emphasis: Being strong with your brain)*

Materials
- Duck, Duck, Goose® board game
- Lucky Ducks® board game

Model the Skill
The teacher models the skill by choosing between two board games.

Guided Lesson
1. Children sit in a circle on the floor.
2. The teacher picks one child to be the "chooser."
3. The chooser decides between the two board games.
4. The chooser decides which peer gets which color of the board game pieces.
5. The teacher leads the game.
6. Repeat so that all children have the chance to be the chooser.

Reinforcers
Children are reinforced with verbal praise, physical praise (high fives, tickles, hugs, pats on the back, sensory input), tangibles (stickers), and positive facial expressions for doing a great job being strong with their brains.

| **Week 7** | **Asserts Self in Socially Appropriate Ways** |
| **Day 4** | Thursday — Obstacle Course *(Emphasis: Being strong with your body)* |

Materials

- Slide
- Bikes
- Chalk

Model the Skill

The teacher models the skill by completing an obstacle course.

Guided Lesson

1. The obstacle course targets each child's difficulties in gross motor skills. It can vary and consist of:
   a. Riding a bike to an area marked with an 'X'.
   b. Jumping three times.
   c. Running up the ladder and down the slide.
   d. Carrying a ball to the finish line.
2. Children sit in a row on the bench in the playground.
3. Children take turns going through the obstacle course.
4. The other children cheer while one child goes through the course.
5. The teacher can help and support children if they struggle through the physical challenges so that they can feel accomplished by completing the course.
6. As each child completes the course, have them pose to show how strong their bodies are.

Indoor Option

The outdoor obstacle course may be substituted with classroom exercise stations. Stations may include jumping jacks, running in place, hopping on both feet, and hopping on one foot.

Reinforcers

Children are reinforced with verbal praise, physical praise (high fives, tickles, hugs, pats on the back, sensory input), tangibles (stickers), and positive facial expressions for doing a great job being strong with their bodies.

Week 7 Asserts Self in Socially Appropriate Ways
Day 5 Friday — Pointing/Word Game *(Emphasis: Being strong with your body)*

Materials

- Three toys (each toy must possess different descriptive characteristics: color, size)
- Three chairs

■ Round 1

Model the Skill

The teacher tells the children, "Today we will be strong with our bodies by showing people what we are looking at. We will point with a strong body." Model the pointing by standing strong and pointing clearly to an object near-by. Check for understanding by having another teacher ask the children, "Will someone get up and touch the thing the teacher is pointing at?"

Guided Lesson

1. Children sit in a row on the floor.
2. The teacher places three chairs significantly spaced apart in front of the children.
3. The teacher places a toy on each chair.
4. Children take turns coming to the center.
5. The teacher whispers the name of a toy into the child's ear.
6. The child must point to the appropriate toy.
7. The teacher asks the other children what the child was pointing to by allowing a particular child to get up and touch the item.

■ Round 2

Model the Skill

After Round 1, the teacher says, "Great job! Now it gets harder! We will now show our friends what we are looking at by pointing and telling them with a strong body and voice." Emphasize by modeling standing strong, pointing clearly, and speaking with one descriptive word for the object. Another teacher asks the children, "Will someone get up and touch the object the teacher is pointing to and describing?"

Guided Lesson

1. Children sit in a row on the floor.

2. The teacher places three similar toys (e.g., three teddy bears) on top of a high cabinet. The toys are placed relatively close together.

3. Children take turns coming to the center.

4. The teacher whispers the name of a toy into the child's ear.

5. The child must point to the appropriate toy.

6. Since the toys are placed relatively close together and they are similar, children must also use one descriptive word to distinguish the appropriate toy (e.g., brown bear).

7. The teacher asks the other children what the child was pointing to and describing.

Reinforcers

Children are reinforced with verbal praise, physical praise (high fives, tickles, hugs, pats on the back, sensory input), tangibles (stickers), and positive facial expressions for doing a great job being strong with their bodies and their words.

Week 7 Asserts Self in Socially Appropriate Ways
Generalization Ideas For The Classroom

Generalizing "Be Strong"

- Take social walks and say "hello" to people whom you pass in school. Encourage children to "be strong" and say "hello" with a loud voice.

- Select one child as a leader for the day and give them a plastic toy microphone to use.

- Outside on the yard, have children call to others by name during games, in transitions, and during clean-up for repeated practice using and hearing their loud voice throughout the day. They are being reinforced for being a leader with their voice and body.

Books

- Snow, Todd. *You Are Brave.* Illus. Melodee Strong. Maren Green Publishing, Inc., 2008.

- Shapiro, Lawrence E. *It's Time to Start Using Your Words.* Illus. Hideko Takahashi. New Harbinger Publications, 2008.

- Cohen, Miriam. *Say Hi, Backpack Baby!* Star Bright Books, 2002.

- Hall, Kirsten. *Duck, Duck, Goose! (My First Reader).* Illus. Laura Rader. Children's Press, 2004.

- Dickson, Anna. *Don't Be Shy: Sesame Street Growing Up Books.* Illus. Tom Cook. Golden Press, 1987.

- Dr. Seuss. *What Was I Scared Of?* Little Dipper Books, 1997.

Category 2 Basic Initiation Skills

- **Week 1** **Expresses Affection Towards a Peer (30 months)**
  Children will learn how to express feelings towards a peer.

- **Week 2** **Shows Pride in Achievements (30 months)**
  Children will learn how to express self-pride verbally.

- **Week 3** **Shares Toys When Prompted (36 months)**
  Children will learn to share when prompted by teachers or peers.

- **Week 4** **Begins to Engage in Associative Play (36 months)**
  Children will participate in similar or identical activities without formal organization, group direction, group interaction, or a definite goal.

- **Week 5** **Shares Divisible Items (36 months)**
  Children will learn how to pass out multiple toys of the same type to their peers.

- **Week 6** **Describes to Others What He/She is Doing (54 months)**
  Children will learn how to describe what they are doing.

- **Week 7** **Calls Attention to Own Performance (54 months)**
  Children will learn how to call attention to their own performance by showing their peers how to copy their actions.

- **Week 8** **Shares Materials and Equipment (60 months)**
  Children will learn how to share playground equipment or classroom supplies/games with their peers.

Week 1 | Expresses Affection Towards a Peer
"Showing Friends How You Feel"

Behavioral Objective

Children will learn how to express how they are feeling.

Identify the Skill Components

- Language
- Emerging or mastered ability to identify basic emotions (in pictures, in scenarios, in real life)
- Ability to imitate emotion from others

Lessons and Materials for the Week

Day	Lesson	Materials
Monday	Greetings	A large blanket, carpet squares
Tuesday	"I Like You"	Scooter boards, balance beam, crash pit
Wednesday	"I'm Proud of You"	Coins, hockey stick, hockey puck, small garbage can
Thursday	Hide and Seek	None
Friday	Freeze Tag	None

For the Parents

Dear Parents,

This week, our social skill classroom behavior is:

Category 2: Basic Initiation Skills	
Week 1	Expresses Affection Towards a Peer "Showing Friends How You Feel"

The development of friendship is important for every child. A crucial element to making friends is showing them that you like and appreciate them. This week, we are targeting specific ways that kids can show each other affection and be caring.

Please encourage your child to express how he/she feels when you do something nice for him/her. Ask your child to show you how he/she feels in the moment.

Here are some ways to practice this skill at home:
• Upon seeing your child, say, "I'm so glad to see you!"
• Have everyone in the family practice using appreciative words such as "Thank you!" and "I'm so glad you helped me!"
• Encourage your child to show you something that he/she accomplished and say, "I'm so proud of you!"

Week 1	Expresses Affection Towards a Peer
Day 1	Monday — Greetings

■ Introduction to the Topic

"This week, we are going to practice showing friends how we feel."

Materials

- A large blanket
- Carpet squares

Model the Skill

Place the carpet squares three feet apart. Teacher A sits on one carpet square while Teacher B sits on the other, both facing each other. Two other adults (or children) hold a blanket vertically like a curtain between the two teachers. When the blanket is dropped to the floor, the teachers can see each other. They say, "Hi ___! I'm glad to see you!"

Guided Lesson

1. Children are divided onto two sides.
2. Two teachers hold up a blanket like a curtain.
3. Two children are chosen to come and sit on carpet squares facing each other on either side of the blanket. The children not participating do not know who was chosen on the other side of the blanket so it will be a surprise for them as well when the blanket is dropped.
4. Teachers drop the blanket.
5. Children are prompted to say, "Hi____! I'm glad to see you!" with a smile.
6. The blanket is raised and new children are selected to sit in front of the blanket.
7. Teachers can encourage funny faces, racing to say hello first, and lots of laughter.

Reinforcers

Children are reinforced with verbal praise, physical praise (high fives, tickles, hugs, pats on the back, sensory input), tangibles (stickers), and positive facial expressions for showing friends their feelings.

Week 1 Expresses Affection Towards a Peer
Day 2 Tuesday — "I like you"

Materials

- Scooter boards
- Balance beam (can be created by placing wooden blocks on the floor)
- Crash pit (can be created by placing several stuffed animals on the floor)

Model the Skill

Teachers create an obstacle course. Teacher A helps Teacher B through the obstacle course. At the end, Teacher A tells Teacher B, "I like you."

Guided Lesson

1. Two children start the obstacle course with the scooter boards. Children are prompted to wait for each other.
2. One child helps the other child on the balance beam.
3. When they finish, the children wait for each other and then crash into the crash pit together.
4. At the end they say, "I like you" to one another.

Reinforcers

Children are reinforced with verbal praise, physical praise (high fives, tickles, hugs, pats on the back, sensory input), tangibles (stickers), and positive facial expressions for showing friends their feelings.

<table>
<tr><td>**Week 1**</td><td>**Expresses Affection Towards a Peer**</td></tr>
<tr><td>**Day 3**</td><td>Wednesday — "I'm Proud of You"</td></tr>
</table>

Materials

- Coins: one per child
- Hockey stick
- Hockey puck
- Small garbage can
- Any materials needed for alternative activities, such as hula hoop, jump rope, bean bags

Model the Skill

Teacher A participates in an activity successfully and then Teacher B says, "I'm proud of you!" and gives Teacher A a high five.

Guided Lesson

◼ Round 1

1. Children sit at a table.
2. Children practice trying to spin a coin.
3. When a child is successful, all the other children are prompted to say, "I'm proud of you!" and give the child a high five.

◼ Round 2

1. Children sit in a line on the floor.
2. Children practice trying to hit a hockey puck into the overturned trashcan "goal."
3. When a child is successful, all the other children are prompted to say, "I'm proud of you!" and give the child a high five.

Reinforcers

Children are reinforced with verbal praise, physical praise (high fives, tickles, hugs, pats on the back, sensory input), tangibles (stickers), and positive facial expressions for showing friends their feelings.

Week 1	Expresses Affection Towards a Peer
Day 4	Thursday — Hide and Seek

Materials

- None

Model the Skill

Teacher A hides. Teacher B shows excitement (e.g., high five, pat on the back, hug) when he/she finds Teacher A.

Guided Lesson

1. Children sit in a row on the floor.

2. One child hides and another child looks for him/her.

3. When the child finds the peer, he/she shows excitement by giving high fives, pats on the back, or hugs.

Indoor Option

Instead of hiding themselves, children can hide small toys in the classroom.

Reinforcers

Children are reinforced with verbal praise, physical praise (high fives, tickles, hugs, pats on the back, sensory input), tangibles (stickers), and positive facial expressions for showing friends their feelings.

Week 1	**Expresses Affection Towards a Peer**
Day 5	Friday — Freeze Tag

Materials

- None

Model the Skill

Model by having Teacher A play against Teachers B and C. Teacher A freezes Teacher B. Teacher B calls out to Teacher C to unfreeze him/her. Teacher B thanks Teacher C for helping him/her.

Guided Lesson

1. Teachers play against the children.
2. The teacher catches children and freezes them.
3. Have extra adults make sure kids stay frozen and call to their unfrozen peers.
4. Have extra adults help the unfrozen children tag the frozen ones.
5. Make sure that the children who get unfrozen express gratitude to the person who unfroze them using smiles, high fives, or handshakes.

Reinforcers

Children are reinforced with verbal praise, physical praise (high fives, tickles, hugs, pats on the back, sensory input), tangibles (stickers), and positive facial expressions for showing friends their feelings.

Week 1 | Expresses Affection Towards a Peer
Generalization Ideas For The Classroom

Generalizing "Showing Friends How You Feel"

- Morning Greetings: Encourage the children to greet each other not only by saying "Hi" but also, "I'm glad to see you!"

- Warm Fuzzies: At the end of the day, have children think about something nice a peer did for them and how it made them feel. These good deeds are called "warm fuzzies" and are quantified by a small token (e.g., sticker, craft fuzz ball) per good deed. The child then puts the warm fuzzy into a jar and the class tries to fill it up.

- Buddies: Pair children up in the classroom. At the end of each activity, have each child compliment the other on how they did on the activity.

Books

- Curtis, Jamie Lee. *Today I Feel Silly and Other Moods That Make My Day.* Illus. Laura Cornell. HarperCollins, 1998.

- Kachenmeister, Cheryl. *On Monday When It Rained.* Houghton Mifflin Harcourt, 2001.

- Cain, Janan. *The Way I Feel.* Parenting Press, 2000.

- Aliki. *Feelings.* Greenwillow Books, 1986.

Week 2	**Shows Pride in Achievements**
	"I Did It!"

Behavioral Objective

Children will learn how to express self-pride verbally.

Identify the Skill Components

- Language
- Ability to comprehend pride
- Ability to identify pride in peers

Lessons and Materials for the Week

Day	Lesson	Materials
Monday	Playground Activities	Slide, balls, basketball hoop
Tuesday	Don't Spill the Beans® Game	Don't Spill the Beans® board game
Wednesday	Wiggle Giggle™ Game	Wiggle Giggle™ board game
Thursday	Bubbles	Pipe cleaners, straws, string, large bubble dish, bubble solution
Friday	Puzzles	1 small puzzle per child, 1 large floor puzzle

For the Parents

Dear Parents,

This week, our social skill classroom behavior is:

Category 2: Basic Initiation Skills	
Week 2	Shows Pride in Achievements "I Did It!"

Most people seek approval for a job well done and as adults, it is critical that we acknowledge a child's pride in achievement. A child's simple cry of "I did it!" is a first step in initiating a social interaction with another individual. This sharing of emotion teaches children about what we value as a family and a society.

Please encourage children to show you their achievements, both big and small, and help them use the phrase "I did it!" Work together on projects so that you can both say, "We did it!"

Here are some ways to practice this skill at home:
- Pick a self-help skill that the child has almost mastered to work on for the week (e.g., brushing teeth, putting on shoes independently). Encourage the child to say, "I did it!" when he/she accomplishes the task.
- Give your child small chores to do around the house and have the child say, "I did it!" when he/she completes the task.
- Work together with your child on a semi-difficult puzzle and at the end say, "We did it!"

Week 2	**Shows Pride in Achievements**
Day 1	Monday — Playground Activities

■ Introduction to the Topic

"This week, we are going to learn how to show our friends that we are proud of ourselves."

Materials

- Slide
- Balls
- Basketball hoop

■ Round 1

Model the Skill

Teacher A models the skill by saying, "I did it!" after going down the slide.

Guided Lesson

1. Children take turns climbing up to the slide.
2. When the children finish sliding, they are prompted to say, "I did it!"

■ Round 2

Model the Skill

Teacher A models the skill by saying, "I did it!" after kicking the ball.

Guided Lesson

1. Children take turns kicking a stationary or rolling ball.
2. When the child kicks the ball, he/she is prompted to say, "I did it!"

■ Round 3

Model the Skill

Teacher A models the skill by shooting the ball into the hoop and saying, "I did it!" if the basket is made or, "Awww man!" if it's missed.

Guided Lesson

1. Children take turns shooting a ball into a basketball hoop.

2. If the child makes it, he/she is prompted to say "I did it!" If the child does not make it, he/she is prompted to say "Awww man!" and then reminded to "stay cool."

Indoor Option

Playground activities may be substituted with classroom activities such as popping bubbles, bowling, or jumping over wooden blocks of various heights.

Reinforcers

Children are reinforced with verbal praise, physical praise (high fives, tickles, hugs, pats on the back, sensory input), tangibles (stickers), and positive facial expressions for expressing pride in themselves verbally.

Week 2	**Shows Pride in Achievements**
Day 2	Tuesday — Don't Spill the Beans® Game

Materials

- Don't Spill the Beans® Game

Model the Skill

Teacher A models the skill by saying, "I did it!" when he/she successfully puts a bean on Mr. Bean.

Guided Lesson

1. Children sit on the floor around the game.

2. Children take turns putting one or two beans on top of Mr. Bean.

3. Children are prompted to say, "I did it!" when they successfully put a bean on Mr. Bean.

4. Children are prompted to say, "Awww man!" if they make Mr. Bean spill.

Reinforcers

Children are reinforced with verbal praise, physical praise (high fives, tickles, hugs, pats on the back, sensory input), tangibles (stickers), and positive facial expressions for expressing pride in themselves verbally.

Week 2	Shows Pride in Achievements
Day 3	Wednesday — Wiggle Giggle™ Game

Materials

- Wiggle Giggle™ board game

Model the Skill

Teacher A spins the spinner and performs the action. When Teacher A is done, he/she says, "I did it!"

Guided Lesson

1. Children sit on the floor around the game.

2. One child gets to spin the spinner then perform the action.

3. The child is prompted to say, "I did it!" upon completing the action.

Reinforcers

Children are reinforced with verbal praise, physical praise (high fives, tickles, hugs, pats on the back, sensory input), tangibles (stickers), and positive facial expressions for expressing pride in themselves verbally.

Week 2	Shows Pride in Achievements
Day 4	Thursday — Bubbles

Materials

- Pipe cleaners
- Straws
- String
- Large bubble dish
- Bubble solution

Model the Skill

Teacher A makes a bubble wand using the assembled materials, blows a bubble, and says, "I did it!"

Guided Lesson

1. Children assemble their bubble wands using:
   a. Pipe cleaners: Twist into any desired shape, but make sure there is a clear loop into which to blow.
   b. Straws and string: Thread the string through two straws and tie off. To use, stretch the straws apart and blow.
2. Children use their bubble wands to blow bubbles.
3. When the children successfully blow a bubble, they are encouraged to say, "I did it!"

Reinforcers

Children are reinforced with verbal praise, physical praise (high fives, tickles, hugs, pats on the back, sensory input), tangibles (stickers), and positive facial expressions for expressing pride in themselves verbally.

Week 2 | Shows Pride in Achievements
Day 5 | Friday — Puzzles

Materials

- One small puzzle for each child
- One large floor puzzle

Model the Skill

Teacher A puts a piece into a small puzzle and tells Teacher B, "I did it!" For Round 2, Teacher A models putting the first two big puzzle pieces together with the phrase, "I did it!"

Guided Lesson

■ Round 1

1. Children sit together on the floor.
2. Children individually build their puzzles.
3. Children are encouraged to say, "I did it!" each time they put in a piece.

■ Round 2

1. Children sit together on the floor.
2. The teacher passes out pieces of the large floor puzzle to each child.
3. Children work together to put their pieces on the puzzle.
4. Children are encouraged to say, "I did it!" when they put on a piece.
5. When the puzzle is completed, all the children are encouraged to say, "We did it!"

Reinforcers

Children are reinforced with verbal praise, physical praise (high fives, tickles, hugs, pats on the back, sensory input), tangibles (stickers), and positive facial expressions for expressing pride in themselves verbally.

Week 2 | Shows Pride in Achievements
Generalization Ideas For The Classroom

Generalizing "I Did It!"

- Homework: When children turn in their homework, have them say, "I did it!" when they give it to the teacher.

- Cleaning up: Have children clean up their work spaces. When they finish, have them say, "I did it!" to each other.

- Bodies in Motion: Ask the children how they want to show excitement with their bodies. Show them a fun arm pump while yelling, "I did it!" and see if the children can come up with their own body movements to identify pride in their accomplishments. Children can jump in the air or pretend to flex their biceps; encourage them to be creative. Have all the children in your classroom say, "I did it!" by thinking together of a body motion they could do to signify that they did it! Each child could suggest an idea. For example, pump arms in the air with a smile to show others that "I did it!"

- Daily Challenge: Pick a challenging task for each day (e.g., puzzles, tangrams, dominoes). The task selected will depend on the developmental needs of the children in the classroom. Have the students work together to complete the challenge. When children accomplish the challenge, have them express their pride by saying, "We did it."

Books

- Carle, Eric. *The Very Quiet Cricket.* Philomel, 1990.

- Piper, Watty, Doris Hauman, and George Hauman. *The Little Engine that Could.* Grosset & Dunlap, 1990.

- Burton, Virginia Lee. *Kathy and the Big Snow.* Houghton Mifflin Harcourt, 1974.

- Curtis, Jamie Lee. *I'm Gonna Like Me.* Illus. Laura Cornell. HarperCollins, 2002.

Week 3	**Shares Toys When Prompted**

Week 3 Shares Toys When Prompted
"Sharing"

Behavioral Objective

Children will learn to share when prompted by teachers or peers.

Identify the Skill Components

- Ability to understand a peer's request
- Ability to identify items and parts being used
- Ability to give an item to a peer

Lessons and Materials for the Week

Day	Lesson	Materials
Monday	Zingo®	Zingo® board game
Tuesday	Duck, Duck, Goose® Game	Duck, Duck, Goose® board game
Wednesday	Musical Bikes	Chalk, bikes, music
Thursday	Ned's Head™ Game	Ned's Head™ board game
Friday	Show and Tell	Items from home

NOTE:

Friday's lesson involves the child's personal possessions from home.
Be sure to ask parents to bring in the materials listed above in advance.

For the Parents

Dear Parents,

This week, our social skill classroom behavior is:

Category 2: Basic Initiation Skills	
Week 3	Shares Toys When Prompted "Sharing"

Sharing is and always will be a cause of conflict among family members. Whether or not your child has siblings, families still must share household items.

Remind your child frequently that he/she must share everything in the house. Praise your child lavishly when a prized possession is shared with a sibling (even if it is for a very limited time), and remind the child that he/she can always ask for help getting it back.

Here are some ways to practice this skill at home:
• Set up a time with your child when he/she must share a favorite toy with a family member. Start with an easy target (e.g., an adult, Dad) and then encourage your child to pick a more difficult target (e.g., a sibling).
• If your child has difficulty with the above activity, set a timer at the child's eye level to define the amount of time he/she must share the toy for. Gradually increase time demands as your child gets better at sharing.
• Remind your child how it makes people feel when they share.

Week 3	Shares Toys When Prompted
Day 1	Monday — Zingo®

■ Introduction to the Topic

"This week, we are going to learn how to share toys with friends."

Materials

- Zingo® board game

Model the Skill

Teacher A models the skill by sharing game pieces with Teacher B upon Teacher B's request. Teacher A can model the words, "Here you go!"

Guided Lesson

1. Children sit in a circle and Zingo® boards are passed out.
2. The first child gets a Zingo® piece.
3. The children who have the matching picture on their board request the piece.
4. The first child gives the Zingo® piece to a peer and uses the catch phrase, "Here you go!"

Reinforcers

Children are reinforced with verbal praise, physical praise (high fives, tickles, hugs, pats on the back, sensory input), tangibles (stickers), and positive facial expressions for sharing well with friends.

Week 3 Shares Toys When Prompted
Day 2 Tuesday — Duck, Duck, Goose® Game

Materials

- Duck, Duck, Goose® board game

■ Round 1

Model the Skill

Teacher A models the skill by sharing his/her "goose" with Teacher B.

Guided Lesson

1. Children sit in a circle on the floor.
2. Children take turns going around the pond with "mother goose."
3. When a child lands on "goose," he/she shares the "goose" with a peer.

■ Round 2

Model the Skill

Teacher A models the skill by sharing his/her board with Teacher B.

Guided Lesson

1. Children sit in a circle on the floor.
2. Children switch their "nest" boards with one another.
3. Children take turns going around the pond with "mother goose."
4. When a child lands on "goose," he/she shares the "goose" with a peer.

Reinforcers

Children are reinforced with verbal praise, physical praise (high fives, tickles, hugs, pats on the back, sensory input), tangibles (stickers), and positive facial expressions for doing a good job sharing.

Week 3	Shares Toys When Prompted
Day 3	Wednesday — Musical Bikes

Materials

- Chalk (to outline a path)
- Bikes
- Music

Model the Skill

Teacher A models the skill by riding a bike in a circle while the music plays. Teacher B watches and when the music stops, Teacher B requests Teacher A's bike.

Guided Lesson

1. Children sit in a row on a bench.
2. Half the children are assigned a bike to ride in the path. The other half are placed along the path randomly (like obstacles).
3. Children are instructed to ride the bike around the path and the other children while the music plays.
4. When the music stops, the standing children request a bike from a peer that is close to them.

Indoor Option

Bikes may be substituted with scooters.

Reinforcers

Children are reinforced with verbal praise, physical praise (high fives, tickles, hugs, pats on the back, sensory input), tangibles (stickers), and positive facial expressions for sharing bikes with their friends.

Week 3 | Shares Toys When Prompted
Day 4 | Thursday — Ned's Head™ Game

Materials

- Ned's Head™ board game

Model the Skill

Teacher A models the skill by picking an item out of Ned's head and giving it to Teacher B to look at for a limited time.

Guided Lesson

1. Children sit in a circle on the floor.
2. Children take turns picking one item out of Ned's head.
3. Children give their item to a peer to look at for a limited time.

Reinforcers

Children are reinforced with verbal praise, physical praise (high fives, tickles, hugs, pats on the back, sensory input), tangibles (stickers), and positive facial expressions for sharing things with their friends.

Week 3	Shares Toys When Prompted
Day 5	Friday — Show and Tell

Materials

- Items from home

Model the Skill

Teacher A models the skill by allowing Teacher B to look at his/her share item for a limited amount of time. This includes allowing Teacher B to hold the item.

Guided Lesson

1. Children sit in a circle on the floor.
2. Children allow their peers to look at and hold their share item for a limited time.

Reinforcers

Children are reinforced with verbal praise, physical praise (high fives, tickles, hugs, pats on the back, sensory input), tangibles (stickers), and positive facial expressions for sharing their own stuff from home.

Week 3 | Shares Toys When Prompted
Generalization Ideas For The Classroom

Generalizing "Sharing"

- Recess Toys: Limit the number of toys to play with at recess to encourage sharing among classmates.
- Craft Materials: Limit the number of glue bottles and art materials that you place on the table to encourage sharing among classmates.
- Library Time: If you have a school or small classroom library, encourage the children to pair up and find a book. On command, have the children share their books with one another.

Books

- Silverstein, Shel. *The Giving Tree.* HarperCollins, 2004.
- Parker, David. *I Can Share.* Scholastic, Inc., 2005.
- Larsen, Kirsten. *It's Sharing Day!* Illus. Ron Zalme. Simon Spotlight/Nickelodeon, 2007.
- Mayer, Mercer. *Me Too!* Random House Books for Young Readers, 2001.

<table>
<tr><td>**Week 4**</td><td>**Begins to Engage in Associative Play**
"Playing with Friends"</td></tr>
</table>

Behavioral Objective

Associative Play is a form of play in which a group of children participate in similar or identical activities without formal organization, group direction, group interaction, or a definite goal. The children may borrow or lend toys or pieces of play materials, and they may imitate others in the group, but each child acts independently, as occurs on a playground or among a group riding tricycles/bicycles. This week, children will learn to engage in associative play.

Identify the Skill Components

- Language
- Ability to maintain eye contact
- Acknowledgement of peers
- Ability to maintain attention
- Cognitive capacity to play appropriately with materials

Lessons and Materials for the Week

Day	Lesson	Materials
Monday	Painting	Paint, large sheet of butcher paper, vegetables
Tuesday	Legos®	Legos®
Wednesday	Puzzles	Puzzles
Thursday	Chase	None
Friday	Coloring	Crayons, Dot-a-Dot™ art, butcher paper

For the Parents

Dear Parents,

This week, our social skill classroom behavior is:

Category 2: Basic Initiation Skills	
Week 4	Begins to Engage in Associative Play "Playing with Friends"

This week's activities all involve the children playing one game or participating in one activity together and acknowledging each other during the activity.

At home, encourage your child to associate themselves with their siblings and/or similar-aged neighbors by having them work together to make something.

Here are some ways to practice this skill at home:
• Bake a cake and have everyone in the family decorate it together; acknowledge that everyone is doing it together.
• Have a family movie night and collaborate to select a film to watch together.
• Go to a nearby park and make a pact that the family will play on particular park equipment together, taking turns picking what you will do. For example, all family members will use the swings at the same time, or all family members will go down the slide at the same time.

Week 4 Begins to Engage in Associative Play
Day 1 Monday — Painting

Introduction to the Topic

"This week, we are learning how to play with friends."

Materials

- Paint
- One large sheet of butcher paper
- Vegetables (one per child)

Model the Skill

Teacher A and Teacher B paint a picture together using the vegetables as paintbrushes.

Guided Lesson

1. Children sit in a circle on the floor.
2. The teacher places a sheet of butcher paper in the center.
3. The teacher passes one vegetable to each child.
4. Children paint one picture together using the vegetables.

Reinforcers

Children are reinforced with verbal praise, physical praise (high fives, tickles, hugs, pats on the back, sensory input), tangibles (stickers), and positive facial expressions for playing together and making a huge picture.

Week 4 Begins to Engage in Associative Play
Day 2 Tuesday — Legos®

Materials

- Legos®

Model the Skill

Teacher A and Teacher B each make their own tower of Legos® using a particular color or colors. The pieces are strewn along the floor. Teachers model asking each other for the colors they need to build their own tower saying, "Can I please have the blue one?"

Guided Lesson

1. Children sit in a circle on the floor.
2. The teacher divides the group into pairs and assigns colors.
3. Each pair builds a tower out of their colors and asks peers for the pieces they need using appropriate language: "Can I please have___," or "May I please____," or "Please give me___."

Reinforcers

Children are reinforced with verbal praise, physical praise (high fives, tickles, hugs, pats on the back, sensory input), tangibles (stickers), and positive facial expressions for playing together with toys and for helping/talking to each other.

Week 4	Begins to Engage in Associative Play
Day 3	Wednesday — Puzzles

Materials

- Puzzles

Model the Skill

The puzzle pieces are divided in half and Teacher A asks Teacher B for the correct piece to fill in the puzzle.

Guided Lesson

1. Children sit in a circle on the floor.
2. The teacher divides the group into pairs.
3. Each pair gets one puzzle.
4. The teacher divides the puzzle pieces among the pairs.
5. Each child must ask his/her partner for the correct pieces to fill in the puzzle.

Reinforcers

Children are reinforced with verbal praise, physical praise (high fives, tickles, hugs, pats on the back, sensory input), tangibles (stickers), and positive facial expressions for playing with puzzles together.

Week 4 | Begins to Engage in Associative Play
Day 4 | Thursday — Chase

Materials

- None

Model the Skill

Teacher A chases after Teacher B and says, "I got you." Teacher B chases after Teacher A and says "I got you."

Guided Lesson

1. Children sit in a row on a bench.
2. Each child takes turns running and having another child chase him/her.
3. Children are encouraged to say, "I got you" when they catch their peer.
4. Repeat activity until the children have all had the opportunity to chase and be chased.

Indoor Option

Running/chasing may be substituted with walking quickly.

Reinforcers

Children are reinforced with verbal praise, physical praise (high fives, tickles, hugs, pats on the back, sensory input), tangibles (stickers), and positive facial expressions for playing together.

Week 4	**Begins to Engage in Associative Play**
Day 5	Friday — Coloring

Materials

- Crayons
- Dot-a-Dot™ Art markers
- Butcher paper

Model the Skill

Teacher A and Teacher B color one large picture on butcher paper using both the crayons and the Dot-a-Dot™ markers. Teacher A can ask Teacher B for particular colors or supplies using the language, "Can I please have____?"

Guided Lesson

1. Children sit together in pairs.
2. The teacher gives each pair one piece of butcher paper with a large drawing on it (e.g., a big tree or a house). One child can have the crayons, and the other child can have the Dot-a-Dot™ markers.
3. Children color, Dot-a-Dot™, and decorate the drawing together. Children are encouraged to ask their partners to share and switch their coloring supplies.
4. Teachers should circulate and comment on how nicely the children are sharing supplies and coloring their pictures together.

Reinforcers

Children are reinforced with verbal praise, physical praise (high fives, tickles, hugs, pats on the back, sensory input), tangibles (stickers), and positive facial expressions for coloring a beautiful picture together.

Week 4 | Begins to Engage in Associative Play
Generalization Ideas For The Classroom

Generalizing "Playing with Friends"

- Friendship Monitor: Designate a small group of children to be Friendship Monitors during recess and have them make sure that everyone is playing with a friend. Every child should get a turn being the Friendship Monitor this week.

- Conversations with Peers: During activities when the whole class is together (e.g., lunch), encourage children to ask each other what they are doing (e.g., "What do you have for lunch?").

- Partners: Assign children partners for the week. Have children walk with their partners, ask each other questions during snack/lunch, and share supplies during art.

Books

- Parker, David. *I'm a Good Friend!* Illus. Cristina Ong. Scholastic, 2004.

- Meiners, Cheri J. *Join In and Play.* Free Spirit Publishing, 2003.

- Carle, Eric. *A House for Hermit Crab.* Simon & Schuster Children's Publishing, 2009.

- Baines, Rachel. *The Playful Little Fairy.* DK Publishing, 2008.

Week 5 | Shares Divisible Items
"Share Toys"

Behavioral Objective

Children will learn how to pass out multiple toys of the same type to their peers.

Identify the Skill Components

- Ability to understand a peer's request
- Ability to identify items and parts being used
- Ability to give another item to a peer

Lessons and Materials for the Week

Day	Lesson	Materials
Monday	Play Dough Toys	Play dough, play dough toys (rolling pins, cookie cutters), utensils (knives, scissors, etc.)
Tuesday	Picture Frame Activity	Cardboard frames, glue, decorative materials, crayons and markers
Wednesday	Modified Poker	Deck of cards, poker chips
Thursday	Apple, Apple, Orange!	Toy apples, one toy orange
Friday	Oreo Matchin' Middles™ Game	Oreo Matchin' Middles™ board game

For the Parents

Dear Parents,

This week, our social skill classroom behavior is:

Category 2: Basic Initiation Skills	
Week 5	Shares Divisible Items "Share Toys"

This week, all of our activities involve sharing, but unlike "*Sharing*" introduced in Week 3, this week, we will be sharing multiple items of the same kind. Furthermore, we will practice passing out items and not receiving anything in return.

At home, have your child practice passing various items out to family members. To challenge your child further, encourage him/her to share favorite items if there are multiples of the same toy (e.g., Hot Wheels cars).

Here are some ways to practice this skill at home:
- Have your child set the table and practice passing out the napkins, forks, spoons, and knives to family members.
- Have your child help you put lunches together for everyone in the family. Your child must "share" the sandwiches, juices, and cookies with family members.
- Encourage your child to share favorite toys with parents, siblings, and grandparents and play together as a family.
- Play tea party with your child and have the child practice passing out items to his/her imaginary friends.

Week 5 Shares Divisible Items
Day 1 Monday — Play Dough Toys

■ Introduction to the Topic

"This week, we are going to learn to share toys with our friends by asking them, 'Can you please share___?' or by giving them something they asked for."

Materials

- Play dough
- Play dough toys (rolling pins, cookie cutters)
- Utensils (knives, scissors)

Model the Skill

Teacher A has all the cutters and Teacher B has all the play dough colors. Teacher A has to ask Teacher B for a play dough color while Teacher B has to ask Teacher A for a cutter/shape. Teachers can model requesting by using the language, "Can you please share the___?"

Guided Lesson

1. One child has all of the play dough colors.

2. One child has all of the cookie cutters.

3. One child has all of the utensils (knives, scissors).

4. Children must request items from one another and share the common materials. Teachers can remind the children to use the catch phrase, "Can you please share the___?"

Reinforcers

Children are reinforced with verbal praise, physical praise (high fives, tickles, hugs, pats on the back, sensory input), tangibles (stickers), and positive facial expressions for sharing.

Week 5	Shares Divisible Items
Day 2	Tuesday — Picture Frame Activity

Materials

- Cardboard frames
- Glue
- Decorative materials (sequins, glitter, stickers)
- Crayons and markers

Model the Skill

Teacher A has the sequins while Teacher B has the stickers (similar to Day 1). Teacher A requests an item from Teacher B by saying, "Can you share a whale sticker please?" Teacher B says, "Sure," and hands the sticker to Teacher A. Teacher A can then place the sticker on the cardboard frame. Teacher B can repeat the model by asking Teacher A for some sequins.

Guided Lesson

1. One child has the cardboard frames and one kind of decorative material so that sharing can continue after the frames are handed out.

2. Other children have some decorative materials (one child has sequins, one child has buttons, one child has tissue paper, one child has stickers, one child has glitter, one child has the crayons and markers, etc.).

3. Children must practice requesting items from one another and sharing the common materials by using the phrase, "Can you share _____ with me?" and responding with "Yes" or "Sure."

Reinforcers

Children are reinforced with verbal praise, physical praise (high fives, tickles, hugs, pats on the back, sensory input), tangibles (stickers), and positive facial expressions for sharing materials.

Week 5 Shares Divisible Items
Day 3 Wednesday — Modified Poker

Materials

- Deck of playing cards
- Poker chips

Model the Skill

Teacher A passes two cards to Teacher B. Teacher B looks at his/her cards to see if there's a match. If the cards match in any way (color, number, or suit), Teacher B says, "I have a match. Can I have a chip?" Teacher A models responding saying, "Yes" or "Sure." The idea is that two children will be sharing and giving out cards and chips to the other children, practicing the act of giving.

Guided Lesson

1. One child is the "dealer" and passes out one card to all the kids and then a second card.

2. Another child is designated as the chip giver.

3. Children look to see if they have a match, either by color, suit, or number. If any child has a match, they get a poker chip by saying, "I have a match. Can I have a chip?"

4. Rotate the dealer and the chip giver so that everyone gets a turn.

Reinforcers

Children are reinforced with verbal praise, physical praise (high fives, tickles, hugs, pats on the back, sensory input), tangibles (stickers), and positive facial expressions for sharing cards with others.

Week 5	Shares Divisible Items
Day 4	Thursday — Apple, Apple, Orange!

Materials

- Toy apples
- One toy orange

Model the Skill

Three teachers sit in a circle. Teacher A passes the apples and orange out to the other teachers. The teacher that receives the orange chases Teacher A. The focus is on children handing out objects to others, thereby practicing the act of giving.

Guided Lesson

1. Children sit in a circle.
2. The child who is "It" passes out the objects.
3. The child who receives the different item (i.e., the orange) has to chase the "It" child.
4. Children take turns being "It."

Reinforcers

Children are reinforced with verbal praise, physical praise (high fives, tickles, hugs, pats on the back, sensory input), tangibles (stickers), and positive facial expressions for sharing.

Week 5	**Shares Divisible Items**
Day 5	Friday — Oreo Matchin' Middles™ Game

Materials

- Oreo Matchin' Middles™ game

Model the Skill

Teachers A and B take the bottom sides of the Oreos and put the matching topsides into a container. Teacher A reaches into the container and pulls out a topside. If it matches Teacher B's indented side, Teacher A hands it to him/her saying, "Here's your shape!" Teacher B can also say, "That shape matches mine. Can you share it?"

Guided Lesson

1. The purpose of the modified game is to have children identify if the item they chose belongs to them or a peer, and then to pass it to the peer when appropriate.
2. Pass out the bottoms of all cookies and put the topsides into a container.
3. Children take turns picking out the tops from the container.
4. The children identify if the piece matches their topside or a peer's.
5. If it matches a peer's, the child who picked it can say, "Here's your shape." If the peer notices the match first, the peer can say, "That shape matches mine. Can you share?"

Reinforcers

Children are reinforced with verbal praise, physical praise (high fives, tickles, hugs, pats on the back, sensory input), tangibles (stickers), and positive facial expressions for sharing shapes with friends.

Week 5 | Shares Divisible Items
Generalization Ideas For The Classroom

Generalizing "Share Toys"

- Art: Have children bring in art supplies to share. During art time, have the children go to their cubbies and get their art materials. Have them share their own materials with the class.

- Art: You can also assign children a particular art material for the week that they must share with the class upon request. For example, one child is the crayon monitor and keeps the box in a special place he/she chooses, but must retrieve it when asked.

- Classroom Materials: As with the art supplies, you can do the same with many classroom materials (e.g., carpet squares, calendar items, scissors). Assign specific materials to a particular child or group for the week so that they must get what the classmates need and distribute them. Again, facilitate and practice the act of passing and sharing things with others.

Books

- Pfister, Marcus. *The Rainbow Fish.* Trans. J. Alison James. North-South Books, 1992.

- Badhan-Quallen, Sudipta. *The Mine-o-saur.* Illus. David Clark. Putnam Juvenile, 2007.

- Mayer, Mercer. *I Am Sharing.* Random House Books for Young Readers, 1995.

Week 6	**Describes to Others What He/She is Doing**
	"Tell Friends What You're Doing"

Behavioral Objective

Children will learn how to describe what they are doing; how the other children interpret their peers' actions is not a focus.

Identify the Skill Components

- Awareness of what one is doing
- Ability to verbalize at least two word descriptions
- Ability to imitate peers' actions

Lessons and Materials for the Week

Day	Lesson	Materials
Monday	Beanbag Toss	Beanbags, board with holes
Tuesday	Mystery Picture	Picture with parts (e.g., two scoops of ice cream), different art supplies (crayons, stickers, stamps)
Wednesday	Memory Game	Any memory matching game
Thursday	Exercises	None
Friday	Get Your Sticker	Stickers, ten feet of masking tape

For the Parents

Dear Parents,

This week, our social skill classroom behavior is:

Category 2: Basic Initiation Skills	
Week 6	Describes to Others What He/She is Doing "Tell Friends What You're Doing"

This week, we are working on your child's ability to narrate his/her own play. This is a beginning step for children leading games and creating ideas for expanding cooperative play with peers.

At home, encourage your child to tell you what he/she is doing as often as possible. Know where your child's language ability is and push him/her to describe how to play in as much detail as possible.

Here are some ways to practice this skill at home:
• Let your child pick a familiar game and have him/her explain to the family how to play. Eventually, "sabotage" the game and play in an incorrect way and have your child correct you.
• Let your child teach you how to play a favorite computer game.
• During bath time, follow your child's lead in playing with bath toys and have him/her tell you what to do with the bath toy.

Week 6 Describes to Others What He/She is Doing
Day 1 Monday — Beanbag Toss

■ Introduction to the Topic

"This week, we are practicing how to tell friends what we are doing."

Materials

- Beanbags
- Board with holes

Model the Skill

Teacher A models the skill by first describing how he/she is going to toss the beanbag and then tossing it in that particular manner.

Guided Lesson

1. Children sit in a row on the floor.
2. Children describe how they are going to toss their beanbag. For example: "I'm going to take two steps and spin," or, simply, "I hop." (Children may initially need suggestions on how they can toss the beanbag.)
3. Children toss the beanbag.
4. Other children imitate their peers' actions.

Reinforcers

Children are reinforced with verbal praise, physical praise (high fives, tickles, hugs, pats on the back, sensory input), tangibles (stickers), and positive facial expressions for describing their actions.

Week 6 Describes to Others What He/She is Doing
Day 2 Tuesday — Mystery Picture

Materials

- Picture with parts (e.g., two scoops of ice cream)
- Different art supplies (crayons, stickers, stamps, sequins)

Model the Skill

Teacher A models the skill by describing how he/she is decorating a picture.

Guided Lesson

1. Children sit in a circle at the table.
2. Children all receive the same picture.
3. Children all receive the same art supplies.
4. One child picks one art supply and one part of the picture.
5. The child instructs the others by describing what he/she is doing: "I'm stamping the ice cream cone." (The focus is on the child giving the instructions. If a child needs assistance processing what the instructing child said, it is acceptable for the teacher to show the child—preferably nonverbally—what he/she should do).
6. Other children imitate their peer's action.
7. Repeat so that all children have the opportunity to pick a part of the picture and art supply, and describe their action.

Reinforcers

Children are reinforced with verbal praise, physical praise (high fives, tickles, hugs, pats on the back, sensory input), tangibles (stickers), and positive facial expressions for describing their actions.

Week 6 Describes to Others What He/She is Doing
Day 3 Wednesday — Memory Game

Materials

- Memory-matching game

Model the Skill

Teacher A describes the two pictures he/she chose: "I found a ___ and a ___."

Guided Lesson

1. Children sit in a circle on the floor.

2. Each child chooses two pictures.

3. Children describe the two pictures they chose: "I found a horse and a duck; not a match." For children with less verbal ability, it can be as simple as, "found horse" and "found duck."

Reinforcers

Children are reinforced with verbal praise, physical praise (high fives, tickles, hugs, pats on the back, sensory input), tangibles (stickers), and positive facial expressions for describing their actions.

Week 6 Describes to Others What He/She is Doing
Day 4 Thursday — Exercises

Materials

- None

Model the Skill

Teacher A models the skill by describing an exercise and performing it.

Guided Lesson

1. Children sit in a row on the floor.
2. Children choose an exercise and demonstrate it.
3. Children describe their exercise: "I'm jumping."
4. Other children imitate their peers' actions.

Reinforcers

Children are reinforced with verbal praise, physical praise (high fives, tickles, hugs, pats on the back, sensory input), tangibles (stickers), and positive facial expressions for describing their actions.

Week 6	**Describes to Others What He/She is Doing**
Day 5	Friday — Get Your Sticker

Materials

- Stickers
- Ten feet of masking tape on the floor, placed like a path from where the children sit to where the stickers are

Model the Skill

Teacher A models the skill by acting out and describing how he/she will get to the sticker across the room. For example, Teacher A will hop to the sticker on the masking tape and state, "I'm hopping to the sticker." Teacher A will then take the sticker and place it on him/herself stating, "I'm putting the sticker on my hand."

Guided Lesson

1. Children sit in a row on the floor facing the masking tape that leads to the stickers.

2. The first child describes how he/she will get to the sticker: "I'm going to crawl." (Teachers may need to prompt children with, "Tell friends what you're doing.") The child then goes to the sticker in that manner. The child can then describe where he/she will put the sticker: "I'm putting the sticker on my nose!"

3. Other children imitate their peer's actions both by how they travel to the sticker and where they place the sticker on their body. If a child (not the leader) does not want to imitate the peer in travel method or sticker placement, it is not relevant. Imitating is not the focus of the activity; children describing their actions to their peers is the goal.

4. Repeat so that all children have the opportunity to describe how they will go down the path and where they will place their sticker.

Reinforcers

Children are reinforced with verbal praise, physical praise (high fives, tickles, hugs, pats on the back, sensory input), tangibles (stickers), and positive facial expressions for describing their actions.

Week 6 Describes to Others What He/She is Doing
Generalization Ideas For The Classroom

Generalizing "Tell Friends What You're Doing"

- Free Play: Encourage children to tell their peers what they are playing with. For example, "I'm playing with the Legos®."

- Snack and Lunch: Encourage children to tell their peers what they are eating during snack and lunch.

- Transitions to/from Recess: The line leader should pick a unique way of walking down the hallway and describe to peers what he/she is doing. For example, "I'm skipping."

Books

- Mitton, Tony. *Down By the Cool of the Pool.* Illus. Guy Parker-Rees.

- Dr. Seuss. *Ten Apples Up on Top.* Beginner Books, 1961.

Week 7	**Calls Attention to Own Performance**
	"Teach Friends"

Behavioral Objective

Children will learn how to call attention to their own performance by showing their peers how to copy their actions.

Identify the Skill Components

- Awareness of what one is doing
- Ability to verbalize at least three to four word phrases
- Ability to imitate peers' actions

Lessons and Materials for the Week

Day	Lesson	Materials
Monday	Art Projects	Pre-cut construction paper shapes, glue, paper
Tuesday	Dancing	Music, CD player
Wednesday	Clay	Clay, popsicle sticks or other modeling tools
Thursday	Drawing	Crayons, paper
Friday	Gym Demonstrations	Balls, jump rope, hula hoop, etc.

For the Parents

Dear Parents,

This week, our social skill classroom behavior is:

Category 2: Basic Initiation Skills	
Week 7	Calls Attention to Own Performance "Teach Friends"

This week, we want your child to learn how to draw attention to different aspects of performing a task. Building upon last week's objective of narrating one's own actions, the emphasis this week is on using more detailed descriptions of actions to teach others (as opposed to simple narration).

Encourage your child to talk to you as much as possible, focusing on the specific techniques of his/her performance. For example, if he/she is shooting a basketball, encourage descriptive language of each step in putting your arms under the ball and pushing it up to the hoop. Help your child dissect what he/she is doing using language.

Here are some ways to practice this skill at home:
- At the park, find activities that your child is good at and have him/her teach you or a sibling how to play.
- If your child has a sibling that is a picky eater, encourage your child to demonstrate how to eat the target food.
- Decorate an ice cream sundae and have your child show you how to make your sundae like his/hers.

Week 7	**Calls Attention to Own Performance**
Day 1	Monday — Art Projects

■ **Introduction to the Topic**

"This week, we are learning to show our friends how to do something by saying, 'Look how I ____.'"

Materials

- Pre-cut construction paper shapes (circles, triangles, squares)
- Glue
- Paper

Model the Skill

Teacher A shows Teacher B how to make a picture from the paper shapes by saying, "Look how I glue the triangle on top of the square to make a house."

Guided Lesson

1. Children sit around a table with the art supplies in the middle.
2. One child is selected to be the "teacher."
3. The "teacher" makes an object out of the shapes.
4. The "teacher" explains how to make the object by saying, "Look how I ____."
5. The other children imitate the design.
6. Repeat so that all children have an opportunity to be the "teacher."

Reinforcers

Children are reinforced with verbal praise, physical praise (high fives, tickles, hugs, pats on the back, sensory input), tangibles (stickers), and positive facial expressions for teaching or following their peers.

Week 7 Calls Attention to Own Performance
Day 2 Tuesday — Dancing

Materials

- Music
- CD Player

Model the Skill

Teacher A shows Teacher B how to do a dance to the music by saying, "Look how I move my toes." Teacher B copies Teacher A's dance move.

Guided Lesson

1. Children sit in a semi-circle on the floor.
2. One child is selected to be the leader.
3. The leader does a dance move in front of all the other children.
4. The leader explains how to do the dance by saying, "Look how I _____."
5. The other children copy the leader's dance move.
6. Repeat so that all children have the opportunity to be the leader.

Reinforcers

Children are reinforced with verbal praise, physical praise (high fives, tickles, hugs, pats on the back, sensory input), tangibles (stickers), and positive facial expressions for teaching or following their peers.

Week 7 Calls Attention to Own Performance
Day 3 Wednesday — Clay

Materials

- Clay
- Popsicle sticks or other modeling tools

Model the Skill

Teacher A shows Teacher B how to make a clay sculpture by saying, "Look how I cut my clay." Teacher B copies Teacher A's sculpture.

Guided Lesson

1. Children sit around a table, each with a piece of clay, with the modeling materials in the middle.
2. One child is selected to be the leader.
3. The leader sculpts the clay in front of the other children.
4. The leader explains how to make the sculpture by saying, "Look how I _____."
5. The other children copy the leader's sculpture.
6. Repeat so that all children have the opportunity to be the leader.

Reinforcers

Children are reinforced with verbal praise, physical praise (high fives, tickles, hugs, pats on the back, sensory input), tangibles (stickers), and positive facial expressions for teaching or following their peers.

Week 7 | Calls Attention to Own Performance
Day 4 | Thursday — Drawing

Materials

- Crayons
- Paper

Model the Skill

Teacher A shows Teacher B how to draw a picture by saying, "Look how I drew my sun." Teacher B copies Teacher A's picture.

Guided Lesson

1. Children sit around a table with a piece of paper and crayons.
2. One child is selected to be the leader.
3. The leader draws a simple drawing in front of the other children.
4. The leader explains how to make the drawing by saying, "Look how I _____."
5. The other children copy the leader's drawing.
6. Repeat so that all children have the opportunity to be the leader.

Reinforcers

Children are reinforced with verbal praise, physical praise (high fives, tickles, hugs, pats on the back, sensory input), tangibles (stickers), and positive facial expressions for teaching or following their peers.

Week 7	**Calls Attention to Own Performance**
Day 5	Friday — Gym Demonstrations

Materials

- Balls
- Jump rope
- Other gym materials (e.g., hula hoops)

Model the Skill

Teacher A shows Teacher B how to tumble by saying, "Look how I tuck my head, put my head down on the floor and turn over." Teacher B copies Teacher A's gym move.

Suggested Activities

- Tumbling/somersaults
- Cartwheels
- Shooting a ball into a hoop
- Jumping rope

Guided Lesson

1. Children work with a teacher to figure out what gym demonstration they want to perform.
2. Children sit in a semi-circle on the floor.
3. One child is selected to demonstrate his/her gym move.
4. The leader performs the gym move then explains how to do it by saying, "Look how I _____."
5. The other children copy the leader's move.
6. Repeat so that all children have the opportunity to be the leader.

Indoor Option

Shooting a ball into a hoop may be substituted with shooting a ball into a bucket. Jumping rope may be substituted by jumping over structures of various heights.

Reinforcers

Children are reinforced with verbal praise, physical praise (high fives, tickles, hugs, pats on the back, sensory input), tangibles (stickers), and positive facial expressions for teaching or following their peers.

Week 7 | Calls Attention to Own Performance
Generalization Ideas For The Classroom

Generalizing "Teach Friends"

- Academic Programs: Pick out strengths in each of your children and have them lead an academic activity with their peers who may not be as good at that subject. For example, if a child is strong in addition concepts, have the child lead the class on how to solve an addition problem.

- Gross Motor Programs: During P.E. time, have the children demonstrate their skills playing with different sports equipment and teach the other children how to play with them.

Books

- Carle, Eric. *From Head to Toe.* HarperFestival, 2007.
- Clark, Emma Chichester. *Friends Forever: The Adventures of Melrose and Croc.* Sandy Creek, 2009.

Week 8 | Shares Materials and Equipment
"Recess/Buddies"

Behavioral Objective

Children will learn how to share playground equipment or classroom supplies/games with their peers.

Identify the Skill Components

- Ability to identify items and parts being used
- Ability to give an item to a peer
- Ability to take turns

Lessons and Materials for the Week

Day	Lesson	Materials
Monday	Hopscotch	Chalk, stone
Tuesday	Baton Relay	Two batons
Wednesday	Four Square	Chalk, ball
Thursday	Handball	Chalk, ball
Friday	Kickball	Kickball

For the Parents

Dear Parents,

This week, our social skill classroom behavior is:

Category 2: Basic Initiation Skills	
Week 8	Shares Materials and Equipment "Recess/Buddies"

Resources can be limited everywhere we go and this is especially true in the child's world. This week's activities relate closely to park and outdoor equipment. While most children have their own bikes, other equipment needs to be shared: common playground games often rely on a child's ability to share materials.

This week, please work on your child's ability to share large equipment outside with peers and siblings. Help your child figure out what language to use with his/her peers when there are limited toys to play with. We will be introducing topics such as compromising and trading equipment in class in the upcoming weeks.

Here are some ways to practice this skill at home:
• Take your child to the park and help him/her think of ideas on how to share the different toys there.
• Continue to work on games that we're working on in class: hopscotch, baton relays, handball, four square, and kickball.

<table>
<tr><td>**Week 8**</td><td>**Shares Materials and Equipment**</td></tr>
<tr><td>**Day 1**</td><td>Monday — Hopscotch</td></tr>
</table>

■ Introduction to the Topic

"This week, we are learning how to share toys with our friends during recess."

Materials

- Chalk to draw the hopscotch board
- Stone or other marker

■ Round 1

Model the Skill

To ensure the children know how to go through the course, Teacher A completes the hopscotch course, and then Teacher B does the same. Round 1 is a preparation round.

Guided Lesson

1. Children line up behind the hopscotch course.
2. Children take turns hopping through the course.

■ Round 2

Model the Skill

Teacher A uses the stone to mark which box he/she is going to skip, and then plays hopscotch. Teacher A then passes the stone to Teacher B to allow Teacher B to play. Teacher A uses the phrase, "Here you go, (name)." Given the size of the group, it would be most efficient to draw multiple hopscotch courses and limit the number of children on each course (say, two per course).

Guided Lesson

1. Children line up behind the hopscotch course.
2. One child throws the stone and plays hopscotch.
3. The child picks up the stone and passes it to the next child in line. Children are encouraged to use the phrase, "Here you go, (name)." They can add, "It's your turn."

4. Repeat steps 2 and 3 until all the children have a chance to play.

Indoor Option

Teachers can use masking tape on the floor to create a hopscotch course. Cars, blocks, and toy cups can all be used as markers.

Reinforcers

Children are reinforced with verbal praise, physical praise (high fives, tickles, hugs, pats on the back, sensory input), tangibles (stickers), and positive facial expressions for sharing equipment with their peers.

Week 8 Shares Materials and Equipment
Day 2 Tuesday — Baton Relay

Materials

- Two batons

Model the Skill

Teacher A runs to Teacher B and passes the baton. Teacher B can then run to Teacher C and pass the baton.

Guided Lesson

1. Children are divided into two teams.

2. Children are spread out around a track or course drawn out by the teacher. The children should be facing forward but looking backwards towards the child behind them so they're ready to receive the baton when it's their turn.

3. The first runners from each team are given a baton.

4. The first runners run to the second runners and pass the baton.

5. Children continue to pass batons to their peers until they get to the finish line.

Indoor Option

Batons may be substituted with musical instruments. Divide the children into two teams and have them sit in two lines, passing the musical instrument until they get to the finish line.

Reinforcers

Children are reinforced with verbal praise, physical praise (high fives, tickles, hugs, pats on the back, sensory input), tangibles (stickers), and positive facial expressions for working together and sharing the baton with their peers.

Week 8 Shares Materials and Equipment
Day 3 Wednesday — Four Square

Materials

- Chalk to draw the Four Square court
- Ball

Set Up the Game

Draw one large square (approximately 10ft x 10ft) and divide that square into four smaller squares.

Model the Skill

Four teachers (or a mix of teachers and kids) play Four Square while all the other children wait in line. When someone loses, they give each other high fives and the loser goes to the back of the line.

Guided Lesson

1. Children form a line by the side of the Four Square court.
2. Four children are selected to play Four Square.
3. Children take turns bouncing the ball to one another.
4. The child who does not catch and bounce the ball back before the ball bounces twice is out.
5. The child who is out is prompted to go to the back of the line.
6. The next child in line is invited onto the Four Square court.
7. Steps 3-6 are repeated until all of the children have a chance to play.

Indoor Option

Four Square may be substituted with classroom board games such as Don't Spill the Beans®. The child who spills the beans goes to the end of the line.

Reinforcers

Children are reinforced with verbal praise, physical praise (high fives, tickles, hugs, pats on the back, sensory input), tangibles (stickers), and positive facial expressions for sharing equipment with their peers.

<table>
<tr><td>**Week 8**</td><td>**Shares Materials and Equipment**</td></tr>
<tr><td>**Day 4**</td><td>Thursday — Handball</td></tr>
</table>

Materials

- Chalk to draw the handball court
- Ball

Model the Skill

Teacher A and Teacher B play handball while the children wait in line. When one teacher loses, they give each other high fives and the loser goes to the back of the line.

Guided Lesson

1. Children form a line by the side of the handball court.
2. Two children are selected to play handball.
3. Children must take turns hitting the ball against the wall.
4. The child who does not hit the ball before the ball bounces on the ground twice is out.
5. The child who is out is prompted to go to the back of the line.
6. The next child in line is invited onto the handball court.
7. Steps 3-6 are repeated until all of the children have a chance to play.

Indoor Option

Handball may be substituted with classroom board game such as Don't Break the Ice®. The child who breaks the ice goes to the end of the line.

Reinforcers

Children are reinforced with verbal praise, physical praise (high fives, tickles, hugs, pats on the back, sensory input), tangibles (stickers), and positive facial expressions for playing together and sharing equipment with their peers.

Week 8 Shares Materials and Equipment
Day 5 Friday — Kickball

Materials

- Kickball

Model the Skill

Teacher A rolls the ball to Teacher B and Teacher B kicks the ball.

Guided Lesson

1. Children form a line.
2. One child is selected to be the pitcher.
3. The pitcher rolls the ball to the first child in line.
4. The first child kicks the ball and the pitcher fetches the ball.
5. The pitcher continues to pitch to the rest of the children.
6. After all of the children have a chance to kick, the pitcher is rotated out and a new child is picked to be the pitcher.
7. Repeat steps 2-6 until all of the children have a chance to be the pitcher.

Indoor Option

Kickball may be substituted by rolling a ball while sitting on the floor.

Reinforcers

Children are reinforced with verbal praise, physical praise (high fives, tickles, hugs, pats on the back, sensory input), tangibles (stickers), and positive facial expressions for playing together and sharing equipment with their peers.

Week 8 Shares Materials and Equipment
Generalization Ideas For The Classroom

Generalizing "Recess/Buddies"

- Recess Buddies: Pair the children off and have them practice the skill they learned in the group during recess.

- Novel Recess Equipment: Introduce brand new recess equipment and have the children practice sharing the new toys.

- Sharing Helper Tools: Ask children to come up with ideas on how to make sharing easier. For example, one idea would be to create a schedule of who gets what equipment during recess.

Books

- Carlson, Nancy. *How to Lose All Your Friends.* Puffin, 1997.

- O'Neill, Alexis, and Laura Huliska-Beith. *The Recess Queen.* Scholastic Press, 2002.

Category 3 | Turn Taking and Simple Social Play

- **Week 1** **Takes Turns by Allowing Others to Go First (42 months)**
  Children will learn how to take turns by allowing others to go ahead of themselves.

- **Week 2** **Allows or Offers to Let Others Play With His/Her Toys (42 months)**
  Children will learn how to offer their own possessions to their peers.

- **Week 3** **Asks Permission to Use Belongings of Others (54 months)**
  Children will learn how to ask for others' belongings.

- **Week 4** **Shares and Takes a Turn (60 months)**
  Children will learn how to share common equipment to play a game together.

- **Week 5** **Responds with Appropriate Affect in Frustrating Social Situations (60 months)**
  Children will learn to respond to frustration or disappointment with appropriate affect in a social situation.

- **Week 6** **Accepts Differences in Routines Appropriately (60 months)**
  Children will learn to appropriately accept changes in routines.

- **Week 7** **Responds with Appropriate Affect in Positive Social Situations (60 months)**
  Children will learn to respond with appropriate affect in a positive social situation.

- **Week 8** **Takes Turns on Playground Equipment (72 months)**
  Children will learn how to take turns with playground/classroom equipment by allowing others to go ahead of themselves.

Week 1	Takes Turns by Allowing Others to Go First
	"Take Turns"

Behavioral Objective

Children will learn to take turns by allowing others to go ahead of themselves.

Identify the Skill Components

- Language: telling peers it's their turn
- Ability to follow directions from a peer
- Cognitive capacity to understand that people take turns during activities/ games
- Allows others to go first
- Takes turns with concrete toys
- Allows another child to choose the activity
- Some understanding of socio-dramatic play (ability to pretend)

Lessons and Materials for the Week

Day	Lesson	Materials
Monday	Mr. Mouth® Game	Mr. Mouth® board game
Tuesday	Building Buildings	Legos®
Wednesday	Ball Toss	Balls, bucket, board with holes in it
Thursday	Drive-Thru Play	Bikes for each child, play money, play ice cream menu, play ice cream (optional), chalk/tape
Friday	Grocery Store Play	Toy foods/real snacks, grocer hat, play money, play cash register

For the Parents

Dear Parents,

This week, our social skill classroom behavior is:

Category 3: Turn Taking and Simple Social Play	
Week 1	Takes Turns By Allowing Others to Go First "Take Turns"

Taking turns is a basic social skill that all children must acquire for success in social situations both in and outside of the classroom. It is especially important for children to learn how to take turns by allowing their peers the chance to go before them.

Please encourage your child to take turns with a sibling or other children. If other children are not present, you of course can take part in this social skill as well. Encourage your child to let another person go first.

Here are some ways to practice this skill at home:
- If your child has a sibling, give the target child one bag of chips (or pretzels or crackers), and encourage them to take turns eating the chips. Most importantly, encourage the target child to let the sibling pick the first chip. This can be done with any food item that can be shared. Give the item to the target child but have him/her offer it to the sibling first.
- During dinnertime, each family member should take a food item and offer it to another family member first.
- At the grocery store checkout, have your child offer to let the person behind you go first. Once at the counter, alternate taking items out of the cart and placing them on the counter.
- Any opportunity to allow another to get in front of you and your child in a public place is a great generalization. It may slow you down a bit but it is an excellent model!

Week 1	Takes Turns by Allowing Others to Go First
Day 1	Monday — Mr. Mouth® Game

■ Introduction to the Topic

"This week, we are going to practice taking turns with our friends and allowing our friends to go first."

Materials

- Mr. Mouth® board game

Model the Skill

This board game is designed for four children to play simultaneously. The goal is to shoot flies into the mouth of a frog that rotates in a circle. The object of the lesson is to allow others to go first. Teacher A and Teacher B model the skill by taking a plastic fly of a particular color and placing it on their fly shooter. Teacher A looks at Teacher B and does not release his/her fly. Teacher A states, "You can go first, (name)." From that point on, any time both teachers have the plastic fly on the arm of the toy, they will wait and allow the other to go first (depending on which way the frog mouth is turning, to make it sensible).

Guided Lesson

1. Children sit in a circle at the table.
2. Children take flies of a certain color in their hands to feed the frog.
3. The teacher chooses a child by name only and that child is prompted to say to the child to his right, "Jon, you can go first." (The mouth of the frog is moving to the left).
4. The teacher then says, "Great, Jon will go first, then Max." (Max is the original child the teacher picked).
5. It is likely that Jon will wait for the mouth to open and then try to shoot the fly into the mouth.
6. After Jon's turn, Max is logically next.
7. The teacher then has all the children stop and wait.
8. The pair to Max's left is instructed in the same manner as the mouth of the frog moves to the left.
9. The turn-taking works in pairs of two. The teacher can allow the mouth to go around once or twice and ask the children to wait to ensure that each

child permits the adjacent child to go first.

10. The teacher can rotate the pairs as the mouth moves around.

Reinforcers

Children are reinforced with verbal praise, physical praise (high fives, tickles, hugs, pats on the back, sensory input), tangibles (stickers), and positive facial expressions for allowing their peers to go before them.

Week 1	Takes Turns by Allowing Others to Go First
Day 2	Tuesday — Building Buildings

Materials

- Legos®

Model the Skill

Teacher A and Teacher B model the skill by taking turns, allowing the other teacher to go first by putting on one Lego® at a time to make one structure.

Guided Lesson

1. Children sit in a circle on the floor.

2. The teacher places a large tub of Legos® in the center of the circle.

3. Children are all prompted to select a Lego® of their choice.

4. The teacher calls out a child's name and that child then picks another child to go first by saying, "Tom, you can go first."

5. The child who was picked (Tom) puts a Lego® on, and then the other child puts one on as well. Children take turns putting on one Lego® at a time to build one structure when given the opportunity to go first by another child.

6. The turn-taking works in pairs of two.

7. If the children are waiting and taking turns (e.g., looking at each other and alternating), the activity should continue. If one child is adding too many pieces at once, remind them to stop and wait.

8. As they are building, instruct the children to talk about what they are making.

Reinforcers

Children are reinforced with verbal praise, physical praise (high fives, tickles, hugs, pats on the back, sensory input), tangibles (stickers), and positive facial expressions for allowing their peers to have a turn and go first.

| **Week 1** | **Takes Turns by Allowing Others to Go First** |
| **Day 3** | Wednesday — Ball Toss |

Materials

- Board with holes in it (i.e., beanbag throw boards)
- Balls (preferably each pair of children has 2-3 balls of the same color)
- Bucket

◼ Round 1

Model the Skill

Teacher A holds 2-3 balls. Teacher A allows Teacher B to go first by giving him/her one ball at a time. Teacher A can say, "Here, you go first." Teacher B throws the balls into the holes of the board. Teacher B then goes and retrieves the balls and places them in a bucket. Teacher B then gives Teacher A the balls and says, "Now you can go next."

Guided Lesson

1. Children sit in a row on the floor.
2. The teacher gives half the children 2-3 balls of the same color.
3. Children are paired in groups of two: Child A has the balls and Child B does not.
4. Child A is prompted to say to Child B, "Here, you go first," and then give the balls to Child B.
5. Child B throws and then retrieves the balls.
6. Re-pair the children so that the child who went first has the opportunity to offer another child the chance to go first.

◼ Round 2

Model the Skill

Teacher A models the skill by being the "thrower" and throwing the ball into a bucket. Teacher B models the skill by being the "fetcher" and retrieving the ball for the thrower.

Guided Lesson

1. The group of children is divided evenly into Side A and Side B.

2. Buckets are placed in front of the children on Side A.

3. Children on Side A are given 2-3 balls.

4. Children on Side A are prompted to say to the children on Side B, "Here, you go first." They should then walk over to Side B and give the balls to the children across from them. The children on Side A return to their spots behind the buckets and face their Side B partners.

5. Side B children then toss the balls and try to get them in the buckets.

6. Side A children retrieve the balls.

7. Re-pair the children so that the child who went first has the opportunity to offer another child the chance to go first.

Reinforcers

Children are reinforced with verbal praise, physical praise (high fives, tickles, hugs, pats on the back, sensory input), tangibles (stickers), and positive facial expressions for allowing their peers to go first.

Week 1 | Takes Turns by Allowing Others to Go First
Day 4 | Thursday — Drive-Thru Play

Materials

- Bike for each child
- Play money (single dollars)
- An ice cream menu sign with each ice cream costing a dollar
- Play ice cream (optional – can be imaginary if children are at the appropriate level)
- Chalk/tape to mark a starting line

Model the Skill

The ice cream menu sign is placed near Teacher A in the yard. Teacher A says, "I am the ice cream boy/girl. I have yummy ice cream. Come through my drive-thru!" Teacher B lines up with the children at a defined starting line on his/her bike. Teacher B bikes to the sign and just before reaching Teacher A, stops and selects a child to go first. Teacher B tells the children that they will practice taking turns ordering ice cream but when they get to the sign, they must allow another child to go first by saying, "You can go first!" The child chosen can model going through the drive-thru, ordering an ice cream off the menu, and paying for it. The child then bikes back around and returns to the end of the starting line.

Guided Lesson

1. Children wait at the starting line on their bikes on the playground.
2. The teacher says, "We've been letting each other go first and today, you will pick a friend to go first and we will practice taking turns."
3. The teacher picks a child and that child chooses a friend to be the first person to go through the drive-thru.
4. All the other children ride their bikes through the stand and order ice cream from the "ice cream boy/girl."
5. You can alternate who the ice cream boy/girl is, as well as who gets to choose who goes first.

Indoor Option

Bikes may be substituted with scooters.

Reinforcers

Children are reinforced with verbal praise, physical praise (high fives, tickles, hugs, pats on the back, sensory input), tangibles (stickers), and positive facial expressions for allowing their peers to have a turn.

Week 1 Takes Turns by Allowing Others to Go First
Day 5 Friday — Grocery Store Play

Materials

- Toy foods or real snacks
- Grocer hat
- Play money
- Play cash register

Model the Skill

This activity is similar to Day 4 and the drive-thru game. Children will line up to purchase their items, but allow another child to go before them. To model the skill, Teacher A plays the grocer and sits at a table with the cash register. Teacher B can line the children up behind him/her with items to purchase. Teacher B stops before making the purchase and allows the child behind him/her to go first by stating, "You can go first."

Guided Lesson

1. Items of food (either real or fake) are placed on a shelf or table area.
2. A child or teacher is placed at a table with a pretend cash register.
3. Children are given play money.
4. Children are told to choose one item off the shelf and line up to purchase it.
5. The first child to line up is prompted to allow either one or all of the other children to go first by stating, "You can go first." The teacher can judge whether one or more children can go before the lead child based on the size of the group and the temperament of the lead child.
6. After they have all made a purchase, the children can go to a table and either pretend to or literally eat their item.
7. Small, real snacks (e.g., one cracker or one piece of popcorn) are motivating; children will want to keep purchasing and going through the register.
8. This activity is repeated to allow every child a chance to both give up their spot going first and to be the grocer.

Reinforcers

Children are reinforced with verbal praise, physical praise (high fives, tickles, hugs, pats on the back, sensory input), tangibles (stickers), and positive facial expressions for allowing their peers to go first.

Week 1 Takes Turns by Allowing Others to Go First
Generalization Ideas For The Classroom

Generalizing "Take Turns"

- Weekly Jobs: Pick one job for the week that children will take turns doing. For example, do not assign a weekly line leader; have children take turns being the line leader each day. Similarly, a child could be named the line leader for the day but instead, has to choose another child to go first every time they line up. Thus, the child is not actually the line leader but the line leader who has to give up his/her spot!

- Snack Time: Have children take turns asking for snack items. Larger classrooms may be broken up into smaller snack groups. The teacher should prompt children by asking, "Whose turn is it now to ask for a snack?"

- Circle Time: During morning circle, encourage children to take turns saying "Good Morning" to their peers.

- Work Time: During work time, have children take turns passing out papers to their peers. A different child should pass out the papers each day of the week. The child who does the passing should say to the first recipient, "You get your paper first!" If able, the child can also state the order (second, third, fourth, etc.) and at the end, identify him/herself as "last."

- Washing Hands: When children wash their hands before lunch, encourage them to have their peers take a turn before them.

Books

- Butterfield, Moira. *Jungle Jeep.* Illus. Claire Henley. Parragon Books, 2008.

- Phillips, Trish. *The Greedy Dog.* Little Tiger Press, 2008.

- Murphy, Stuart J. *Give Me Half.* Illus. G. Brian Karas. HarperCollins, 1996.

- Rey, Margaret, H.A. Rey, and Alan J. Shalleck, ed. *Curious George and the Pizza.* Houghton Mifflin, 1985.

- Lagonegro, Melissa. *Sealed with a Kiss.* Illus. Elisa Marrucchi. RH/Disney, 2005.

Week 2	**Allows or Offers to Let Others Play With His/Her Toys**
	"Giving to Friends"

Behavioral Objective

Children will learn how to offer their own possessions to their peers.

Identify the Skill Components

- Recognition of own possessions
- Language: verbalizing "Here you go"
- Ability to pass items to peers

Lessons and Materials for the Week

Day	Lesson	Materials
Monday	Crayons from Home	Child's own set of crayons from home, coloring sheets
Tuesday	Cookie Cutters from Home	Child's own set of cookie cutters from home, edible cookie dough or play dough
Wednesday	Book from Home	Child's own book from home
Thursday	Dress-up from Home	Child's own dress-up accessory from home
Friday	Show and Tell	Child's own toy from home, large bag

NOTE:

This week's lessons all involve the child's personal possessions from home.
Be sure to ask parents to bring in the materials listed above in advance.

For the Parents

Dear Parents,

This week, our social skill classroom behavior is:

Category 3: Turn Taking and Simple Social Play	
Week 2	Allows or Offers to Let Others Play with His/Her Toys "Giving to Friends"

It is important for children to be able to offer their possessions to others. Some children can take turns or share in a structured game, but find it more difficult to offer their possessions during unstructured activities.

Please encourage your child to offer his/her possessions to others. If necessary, remind him/her to use the phrase, "Here you go."

Here are some ways to practice this skill at home:
• If your child has a preferred spot to sit at during dinnertime, encourage him/her to give it up to a sibling or parent.
• Have your child help you make lunch. At the end, have your child offer this lunch to a sibling.
• When your child brings home an art project from school, encourage him/her to offer it to a sibling or to the other parent.
• Encourage your child to offer his/her backpack to a sibling to use for a day.
• If a child gets a treat or something nice, encourage him/her to save it and then offer it to either a parent or sibling.

Week 2 | Allows or Offers to Let Others Play With His/Her Toys
Day 1 | Monday — Crayons from Home

Introduction to the Topic

"This week, we are going to learn how to give our things to our friends."

Materials

- Child's own set of crayons from home
- Coloring sheets

Model the Skill

Teacher A models the skill by offering his/her crayons to Teacher B with the phrase, "Here you go."

Guided Lesson

1. Children sit around the table.
2. The teacher passes out each child's own set of crayons.
3. The teacher passes out a coloring sheet to each child.
4. Children take turns offering their crayons to a peer with the phrase, "Here you go."

Reinforcers

Children are reinforced with verbal praise, physical praise (high fives, tickles, hugs, pats on the back, sensory input), tangibles (stickers), and positive facial expressions for offering their possessions.

Week 2	**Allows or Offers to Let Others Play With His/Her Toys**
Day 2	Tuesday — Cookie Cutters from Home

Materials

- Child's own set of cookie cutters from home
- Play dough or edible dough that can be cooked later (if you want a cooking activity)

Model the Skill

Teacher A models the skill by offering his/her cookie cutters to Teacher B with the phrase, "Here you go."

Guided Lesson

1. Children sit around the table.
2. The teacher passes out each child's own set of cookie cutters.
3. The teacher passes out dough to each child.
4. Children take turns offering their cookie cutters to a peer with the phrase, "Here you go."

Reinforcers

Children are reinforced with verbal praise, physical praise (high fives, tickles, hugs, pats on the back, sensory input), tangibles (stickers), and positive facial expressions for offering their possessions.

Week 2 Day 3	Allows or Offers to Let Others Play With His/Her Toys Wednesday — Book from Home

Materials

- Book from home

Model the Skill

Teacher A models the skill by offering his/her book to Teacher B with the phrase, "Here you go."

Guided Lesson

1. Children sit in a circle on the floor.

2. The teacher passes out each child's book.

3. Children take turns offering their book to a peer with the phrase, "Here you go."

Reinforcers

Children are reinforced with verbal praise, physical praise (high fives, tickles, hugs, pats on the back, sensory input), tangibles (stickers), and positive facial expressions for offering their possessions.

Week 2	Allows or Offers to Let Others Play With His/Her Toys
Day 4	Thursday — Dress-up from Home

Materials

- Dress-up accessory from home

Model the Skill

Teacher A models the skill by offering his/her accessory to Teacher B with the phrase, "Here you go."

Guided Lesson

1. Children sit in a circle on the floor.

2. The teacher passes out each child's dress-up accessory.

3. Children take turns offering their dress-up accessory to a peer with the phrase, "Here you go."

Reinforcers

Children are reinforced with verbal praise, physical praise (high fives, tickles, hugs, pats on the back, sensory input), tangibles (stickers), and positive facial expressions for offering their possessions.

Week 2 Allows or Offers to Let Others Play With His/Her Toys
Day 5 Friday — Show and Tell

Materials

- Toy from home
- Large bag

Model the Skill

Teacher A models the skill by picking his/her toy from the bag, showing the toy to Teacher B, and then giving the toy to Teacher B with the phrase, "Here you go."

Guided Lesson

1. Children sit in a circle on the floor.
2. The teacher puts all of the children's toys in a bag.
3. The teacher pulls out a toy.
4. The owner of the toy comes to the front and shows the toy to his/her peers.
5. Children take turns offering their toy to a peer with the phrase, "Here you go."

Reinforcers

Children are reinforced with verbal praise, physical praise (high fives, tickles, hugs, pats on the back, sensory input), tangibles (stickers), and positive facial expressions for showing and sharing with their friends.

Week 2 Allows or Offers to Let Others Play With His/Her Toys
Generalization Ideas For The Classroom

Generalizing "Giving to Friends"

- Snack: Ask children to bring in their favorite snack from home. Encourage children to take turns offering their snack to a peer with the phrase, "Here you go."

- Free Play: Encourage children to offer their toys to peers using the phrase, "Here you go."

- Work Time: If children have their own pencil boxes, encourage them to offer a pencil (or crayon or scissors) to a peer with the phrase, "Here you go."

- Lunch: Only give a few children napkins. Encourage children to give napkins to peers when they need them with the phrase, "Here you go."

Books

- Becker, Shelly. *Mine! Mine! Mine!* Illus. Hideko Takahashi. Sterling, 2006.

- Meiners, Cheri J. *Share and Take Turns (Learning to Get Along, Book 1).* Free Spirit Publishing, 2003.

- Cummings, Carol. *Sharing is Caring: A Social Skill Lesson.* Illus. Jeri Slevin. Teaching Inc., 1992.

- Willems, Mo. *Don't Let the Pigeon Drive the Bus!* Hyperion Press, 2003.

- Shannon, David. *Too Many Toys.* The Blue Sky Press, 2008.

- Rey, Margaret, and H.A. Rey. *Curious George Goes to a Costume Party.* Houghton Mifflin, 2001.

Week 3 | Asks Permission to Use Belongings of Others
"Ask Friends"

Behavioral Objective

Children will learn how to ask for others' belongings.

Identify the Skill Components

- Recognition of own possessions
- Language: verbalizing "Can I have it?"
- Ability to give up own possessions

NOTE:

The lessons from this week are exactly the same as *Week 2: Allows or Offers to Let Others Play with His/Her Toys*, with a variation in the language to shift the focus from giving to asking.

Lessons and Materials for the Week

Day	Lesson	Materials
Monday	Crayons from Home	Child's own set of crayons from home, coloring sheets
Tuesday	Cookie Cutters from Home	Child's own set of cookie cutters from home, edible cookie dough or play dough
Wednesday	Book from Home	Child's own book from home
Thursday	Dress-up from Home	Child's own dress-up accessory from home
Friday	Show and Tell	Child's own toy from home, large bag

NOTE:

This week's lessons all involve the child's personal possessions from home. Be sure to ask parents to bring in the materials listed above in advance.

For the Parents

Dear Parents,

This week, our social skill classroom behavior is:

Category 3: Turn Taking and Simple Social Play	
Week 3	Asks Permission to Use the Belongings of Others "Ask Friends"

Asking for permission is a skill that children must use in various social situations, and many children need to be taught how to ask to use others' belongings.

Please encourage your child to ask for permission to use others' belongings using the catch phrase, "Can I have it?"

Here are some ways to practice this skill at home:
• If your child has a sibling and each child has a preferred spot to sit at during dinnertime, encourage your child to ask his/her sibling for permission to sit in that designated spot during the meal.
• If your child has a sibling, make a different lunch for each of your children and then have your child ask his/her sibling for the other lunch.
• Encourage your child to ask a sibling or peer if he/she can borrow a favorite toy.
• Play dress-up at home and have your child ask to borrow your clothes.

Week 3	Asks Permission to Use Belongings of Others
Day 1	Monday — Crayons from Home

Introduction to the Topic

"This week, we are going to learn about asking our friends for things."

Materials

- Child's own set of crayons from home
- Coloring sheets

Model the Skill

Teacher A models the skill by asking Teacher B for his/her crayons using the phrase, "Can I have it?"

Guided Lesson

1. Children sit around the table.
2. The teacher passes out each child's own set of crayons.
3. The teacher passes out a coloring sheet to each child.
4. Children take turns asking their peers for their crayons with the phrase, "Can I have it?"

Reinforcers

Children are reinforced with verbal praise, physical praise (high fives, tickles, hugs, pats on the back, sensory input), tangibles (stickers), and positive facial expressions for asking others for their belongings.

Week 3 | Asks Permission to Use Belongings of Others
Day 2 | Tuesday — Cookie Cutters from Home

Materials

- Child's own set of cookie cutters from home
- Play dough or edible dough that can be cooked later (if you want a cooking activity)

Model the Skill

Teacher A models the skill by asking Teacher B for his/her cookie cutters using the phrase, "Can I have it?"

Guided Lesson

1. Children sit around the table.
2. The teacher passes out each child's own set of cookie cutters.
3. The teacher passes out dough to each child.
4. Children take turns asking their peers for their cookie cutters with the phrase, "Can I have it?"

Reinforcers

Children are reinforced with verbal praise, physical praise (high fives, tickles, hugs, pats on the back, sensory input), tangibles (stickers), and positive facial expressions for asking others for their belongings.

Week 3 | Asks Permission to Use Belongings of Others
Day 3 | Wednesday — Book from Home

Materials

- Book from home

Model the Skill

Teacher A models the skill by asking Teacher B for his/her book using the phrase, "Can I have it?"

Guided Lesson

1. Children sit in a circle on the floor.

2. The teacher passes out each child's book.

3. Children take turns asking their peers for their books with the phrase, "Can I have it?"

Reinforcers

Children are reinforced with verbal praise, physical praise (high fives, tickles, hugs, pats on the back, sensory input), tangibles (stickers), and positive facial expressions for asking others for their belongings.

Week 3	Asks Permission to Use Belongings of Others
Day 4	Thursday — Dress-up from Home

Materials

- Dress-up accessory from home

Model the Skill

Teacher A models the skill by asking Teacher B for his/her dress-up accessory using the phrase, "Can I have it?"

Guided Lesson

1. Children sit in a circle on the floor.
2. The teacher passes out each child's dress-up accessory.
3. Children take turns asking their peers for their dress-up accessory with the phrase, "Can I have it?"

Reinforcers

Children are reinforced with verbal praise, physical praise (high fives, tickles, hugs, pats on the back, sensory input), tangibles (stickers), and positive facial expressions for asking others for their belongings.

Week 3 Asks Permission to Use Belongings of Others
Day 5 Friday — Show and Tell

Materials

- Toy from home
- Large bag

Model the Skill

Teacher A pulls out a toy from a large bag. Teacher B models the skill by asking Teacher A for the toy using the phrase, "Can I have it?"

Guided Lesson

1. Children sit in a circle on the floor.
2. The teacher puts the children's toys into a large bag.
3. Children take turns pulling out their toy from the bag and showing it to the class.
4. The other children take turns asking their peers for their toy with the phrase, "Can I have it?"

Reinforcers

Children are reinforced with verbal praise, physical praise (high fives, tickles, hugs, pats on the back, sensory input), tangibles (stickers), and positive facial expressions for asking others for their belongings.

Week 3 | Asks Permission to Use Belongings of Others
Generalization Ideas For The Classroom

Generalizing "Ask Friends"

- Snack: Ask children to bring in their favorite snack from home. Encourage them to take turns asking peers for their snacks with the phrase, "Can I have it?"

- Free Play: Encourage children to ask peers for their toys with the phrase, "Can I have it?"

- Work Time: If children have their own pencil boxes, encourage children to ask their peers for a pencil (or crayon or scissors) with the phrase, "Can I have it?"

- Lunch: Only give a few children napkins. Encourage children to ask their peers for a napkin when they need it.

- Books: Have children go to different classrooms and ask their peers for a book to read during circle time.

Books

- Reynolds, Alison. *Teddy Shares.* Illus. Lee Krutop. Sandy Creek, 2009.

- Reynolds, Alison. *Teddy Helps.* The Five Mile Press Pty. Limited, 2008.

- Numeroff, Laura Joffe. *If You Give a Moose a Cookie.* Illus. Felicia Bond. HarperCollins, 1985.

- Numeroff, Laura Joffe. *If You Give a Moose a Muffin.* Illus. Felicia Bond. HarperCollins, 1994.

- Kleinberg, Naomi. *Please and Thank You: A Book about Manners.* Illus. David Dees. Random House Books for Young Readers, 2008.

- Perkins, Janice, and Mark Perkins. *Ladybug Baby Bug.* AuthorHouse, 2007.

Week 4 | Shares and Takes a Turn
"Pass to Friends"

Behavioral Objective

Children will learn how to share common equipment to play a game together.

Identify the Skill Components

- Language: verbalizing "My turn/Your turn"
- Ability to recognize a peer's request
- Ability to give up own possessions

Lessons and Materials for the Week

Day	Lesson	Materials
Monday	Board Games	Hyper Dash™ board game, Cranium Cariboo™ board game
Tuesday	Relays	Buckets (one per child), sponges
Wednesday	Carnival Games	Three magnetic fishing poles, fish with colored stickers on the bottom to match the color of the poles, inflatable swimming pool or large bucket
Thursday	Water Balloon Game	Water balloons, whistle
Friday	Sports Games	Ball, chalk

For the Parents

Dear Parents,

This week, our social skill classroom behavior is:

Category 3: Turn Taking and Simple Social Play	
Week 4	Shares and Takes a Turn "Pass to Friends"

Sharing and taking turns with common equipment is a social situation that children frequently face. It is important for us to help children learn how to share appropriately and take turns.

You can encourage your child to share and take turns by prompting the use of the catch phrase "your turn/my turn." It is also important to encourage your child to say, "Here (name)," when passing something to someone else. Remind your child to use these phrases when sharing and taking turns with common household items.

Here are some ways to practice this skill at home:
• Place only one tube of toothpaste in the bathroom. If your child has a sibling, encourage siblings to brush their teeth together. If your child does not have a sibling, parents can brush their teeth with the child. Every day, encourage your child to share and take turns with the toothpaste.
• Share and take turns pushing the cart at the grocery store.
• If there is a family pet, encourage your child to share and take turns feeding the pet. Prompt him/her to use the words "your turn/my turn."
• At dinnertime, place items (napkins, utensils, cups, the food) at one end of the table and have your child sit where he/she can continuously pass to the next person at the table.
• If your child has a sibling, have both children share and take turns making their lunch with you.

Week 4	**Shares and Takes a Turn**
Day 1	Monday — Board Games

■ **Introduction to the Topic**

"This week, we are going to learn about sharing and taking turns. If it's your turn, tell your friends, 'My turn.' If it's your friend's turn, tell your friends, 'Your turn.'"

Materials

- Hyper Dash™ game
- Cranium Cariboo™ game

Model the Skill

Teacher A takes a turn with the game piece, and then passes it to Teacher B and says, "Your turn."

Guided Lesson

■ **Hyper Dash™**

1. Children sit in a circle on the floor.
2. One child gets the Hyper Dash™ device and plays the game.
3. That child decides which peer will go next.
4. Child passes the Hyper Dash™ device to the peer saying, "Your turn."
5. Repeat steps 2-4 so that all children get a chance to play and pass to a peer.

■ **Cranium Cariboo™**

1. Children sit in a circle on the floor.
2. One child gets the key and plays the game.
3. That child decides which peer will go next.
4. Child passes the key to a peer saying, "Your turn."
5. Repeat steps 2-4 so that all children get a chance to play and pass to a peer.

Reinforcers

Children are reinforced with verbal praise, physical praise (high fives, tickles, hugs, pats on the back, sensory input), tangibles (stickers), and positive facial expressions for sharing materials.

Week 4	Shares and Takes a Turn
Day 2	Tuesday — Relays

Materials

- Buckets (one per child)
- Sponges

Set Up the Game

Fill half of the buckets with water and leave the other buckets empty. Place the buckets 10 feet away from one another. Place one pair of children by each bucket filled with water.

Model the Skill

Teacher A fills the sponge with water, runs to the empty bucket, and wrings out the sponge into the bucket. Teacher A then passes the sponge to Teacher B and says, "Your turn."

Guided Lesson

1. Children pick a partner and both children stand next to a filled bucket.
2. Child A picks up the sponge, submerges it, and fills it with water.
3. Child A then runs to the empty bucket and wrings it out.
4. Child A then runs back to Child B (who is still standing near the filled bucket) and passes the sponge to Child B saying, "Your turn!" Child B can also say, "My turn!"
5. Child B then submerges the sponge to fill it with water.
6. Child B runs to the empty bucket and wrings it out.
7. Child B returns to the filled bucket and passes the sponge to Child A saying, "Your turn!"
8. This continues until the water has been completely transferred from one bucket to another.

Indoor Option

Sponge may be substituted with a small cup. Water may be substituted with small toys. Have children use a cup to scoop up as many toys as they can, drop it off on the other side of the room, and pass the cup to their partner saying, "Your turn."

Reinforcers

Children are reinforced with verbal praise, physical praise (high fives, tickles, hugs, pats on the back, sensory input), tangibles (stickers), and positive facial expressions for passing to their peers.

Week 4	**Shares and Takes a Turn**
Day 3	Wednesday — Carnival Games

Materials

- Three magnetic fishing poles or fishing nets (each a different color)
- Fish with colored stickers on the bottom to match the fishing poles/nets
- Inflatable swimming pool or large bucket

Model the Skill

Teacher A catches a fish and looks to see if the sticker on the fish matches the color of the pole. If so, Teacher A keeps the fish; if not, he/she throws it back in. Teacher A then passes the fishing pole to Teacher B (who is to the right) and says, "Your turn." Teacher B catches a fish and checks if the sticker matches the fishing pole. If so, Teacher B keeps the fish; if not, he/she throws it back in. Teacher B then passes the fishing pole to Teacher C and says, "Your turn." Teacher C catches a fish and checks the color. The pole continues around the circle of teachers.

Guided Lesson

1. Children stand in a circle around the swimming pool/bucket.
2. The number of children around the pool determines the number of poles/nets needed. There should not be too many inactive children; one rod for every two children is ideal.
3. The fishing poles are distributed to the group. Each child uses a pole to catch a fish.
4. If the color of the fish matches the pole, children can keep the fish. If not, they must throw the fish back.
5. Children pass the fishing poles to the peer to their right and say, "Your turn."
6. About half the children are fishing while the others are watching and waiting for their turn. The poles rotate around the children in a circle.

Indoor Option

Substitute the fishing poles and fish with colored balls and cups. Have children try to throw the colored balls into the matching cups. If they make a match, they can keep the cups. If not, they must put the cup back and pass their ball to the next peer and say, "Your turn."

Reinforcers

Children are reinforced with verbal praise, physical praise (high fives, tickles, hugs, pats on the back, sensory input), tangibles (stickers), and positive facial expressions for sharing the equipment with their peers.

Week 4	Shares and Takes a Turn
Day 4	Thursday — Water Balloon Game

Materials

- Water balloons
- Whistle

Model the Skill

Two teachers stand next to each other. A whistle is blown and Teacher A passes a filled water balloon to Teacher B saying, "Here ___." Teacher B then passes it back to Teacher A saying, "Here ___." After a few seconds, the whistle is blown and whoever has the balloon holds onto it. The teachers then step farther away from each other. Teachers can decide how long they want to model and whether they want to actually throw the balloon and have it break!

Guided Lesson

1. Have the children stand in a close circle.

2. As in previous lessons, base the number of balloons used upon the number of children. You want to have them focused on their peers to their left and right but you don't want it to be chaotic; maybe two balloons for every three children.

3. A teacher blows the whistle to start the game. Children pass the balloon to the right and address their peer by name saying, "Here ___."

4. After a short time, the teacher blows the whistle to stop play. The children step one foot out so there is a small space between each child.

5. The teacher blows the whistle again and the children resume passing the balloon. Be sure to prompt them to call to the child next to them saying, "Here ___."

6. This can continue for as long as the teacher wants or until a balloon pops!

Reinforcers

Children are reinforced with verbal praise, physical praise (high fives, tickles, hugs, pats on the back, sensory input), tangibles (stickers), and positive facial expressions for passing to their peers.

Week 4	Shares and Takes a Turn
Day 5	Friday — Sports Games (Four Square)

Materials

- Ball
- Chalk

Set Up the Game

Draw one large square (approximately 10ft x 10ft) and divide that square into four smaller squares.

Model the Skill

Teacher A stands in one square as teachers and children stand in the other squares. Teacher A bounces the ball to Teacher B and says, "Your turn."

Guided Lesson

1. Four children take their places in each of the four smaller squares. All other children line up and wait to have a turn.
2. One child is given a ball.
3. The child is prompted to bounce-pass the ball to another child and say, "Your turn."
4. Repeat steps 2-3 until all peers get a turn having the ball.
5. Repeat steps 1-4 until all the children have a turn playing Four Square.

Indoor Option

Have children sit instead of stand. Bouncing the ball may be substituted with rolling it.

Reinforcers

Children are reinforced with verbal praise, physical praise (high fives, tickles, hugs, pats on the back, sensory input), tangibles (stickers), and positive facial expressions for sharing the equipment with their peers.

Week 4 Shares and Takes a Turn
Generalization Ideas For The Classroom

Generalizing "Pass to Friends"

- Snack: Put children in pairs, giving one child all of the snacks. Instruct children that Child A is in charge of sharing the snacks equally with Child B. They must take one snack then give one snack to their peer saying, "Your turn/My turn." Remind Child B to make sure Child A says, "My turn," if he/she forgets.

- Playground: If children are using bikes or scooters in the outdoor play area and engaging in free riding, have other children "sign-up" verbally with an adult or peer to use the bike or scooter next. When the first child is finished, encourage him/her to give the vehicle to the next child while saying, "Your turn."

- Washing Hands: Put the children in small groups and allow them to use only one sink. Encourage them to share and take turns by saying, "My turn" or "Your turn."

- Free Play: Set out only one type of a special toy (e.g., a wobble board). Encourage children to share and take turns.

Books

- Katz, Karen. *I Can Share.* Grosset & Dunlap, 2004.

- Rey, Margaret, H.A. Rey, and Alan J. Shalleck, ed. *Curious George Goes Fishing.* Houghton Mifflin, 1998.

- Worth, Bonnie. *Cooking with the Cat.* Illus. Christopher Maroney. Random House Books for Young Readers, 2003.

| Week 5 | Responds with Appropriate Affect in Frustrating Social Situations
"Be Cool" |

Behavioral Objective

Children will learn to respond to frustration or disappointment with appropriate affect in a social situation.

Identify the Skill Components

- Language
- Cognitive understanding of emotions
- Ability to control negative emotions

Lessons and Materials for the Week

Day	Lesson	Materials
Monday	Don't Spill the M&M'S®	Don't Spill the Beans® game, bag of M&M'S®
Tuesday	Gift Exchange	One desirable item (cookies), miscellaneous items (e.g., Lego®, plastic spoon, empty plastic bag, tape holder), paper for wrapping the items
Wednesday	Un-favorite Colors	Colored chalk, black paper
Thursday	Game Play	Fun game (e.g., Hullabaloo®), boring game (teacher's choice)
Friday	"Be Cool" Olympics	Two different-colored stickers, desirable prize, semi-undesirable prize, undesirable prize, helmet/hat, scooter for each team

For the Parents

Dear Parents,

This week, our social skill classroom behavior is:

Category 3: Turn Taking and Simple Social Play	
Week 5	Responds with Appropriate Affect in Frustrating Social Situations "Be Cool"

Children face an array of frustrating or disappointing situations throughout their day. How they respond to these situations has an effect on their self-regulation skills and on how others perceive them.

This week, we're teaching children to BE COOL. When they feel mad, they should not cry but should stay cool and keep playing. Children can be cool by breathing, squeezing their hands, closing their eyes, keeping their body calm and still, and saying to themselves, "Be cool, it's just a game." If the children stay cool, be sure to make good things happen. If they lose their cool, they not only lose the game and the fun, but often get nothing while other children receive a prize/reward.

Please encourage your child to respond with appropriate affect and language ("I'm cool") in frustrating or disappointing social situations. Watch to see if your child starts to get frustrated and cue him/her to "be cool." Offer verbal cues and model how to calm your bodies and be cool. You can model this skill by saying, "I'm being cool," when you're faced with frustrating social situations as well.

In each of the following situations, preempt the disappointing presentation with the verbal cue, "Remember, be cool and good things will happen."

Here are some ways to practice this skill at home:
• Serve your child his/her least favorite foods for dinner sometimes and remind him/her to stay cool and then reward your child with dessert.
• Serve dessert with some meals and eliminate it with others. Remind your child that if he/she is cool on a night without dessert, there will be dessert the following day.
• At the park, ask your child to give up a play item (e.g., swing) to a peer. Make sure the item is a preferred activity and cue the child that if he/she is cool in that situation, you can stay at the park.
• Tell your child that you are going to a preferred location (e.g., park, friend's house), but run a few errands along the way. Encourage your child to "be cool" as you run the errands, reminding him/her that you will end up getting to the preferred location.

Week 5	Responds with Appropriate Affect in Frustrating Social Situations
Day 1	Monday — Don't Spill the M&M'S®

■ Introduction to the Topic

"This week, we are going to learn how to BE COOL. When we feel mad, should we cry?* No! We should stay cool and keep playing. We can stay cool by breathing, squeezing our hands, closing our eyes, keeping our body calm and still, and saying to ourselves, 'Be cool, it's just a game,' as many times as we need. If we stay cool, good things will happen; but if we lose our cool, we will lose the game, lose the fun, and get nothing."

*Substitute with particular negative behaviors for each individual child.

Materials

- Don't Spill the Beans® game, altered to be Don't Spill the M&M'S®
- A bag of M&M'S®

Model the Skill

The teacher models the skill by accidentally spilling the M&M'S®. The teacher says, "Oops, I spilled the M&M'S®. But it's okay—it's just a game. I am going to stay cool! I'm going to breathe (teacher models deep breaths), I'm going to squeeze my hands (model), I'm going to close my eyes and hold my body still (model). I'm going to say to myself, 'Be cool, it's just a game.'"

Guided Lesson

1. Children sit in a circle on the floor with the teacher.
2. Children take turns carefully placing M&M'S® on Mr. M&M'S® head.
3. Every time a child spills the M&M'S®, the other children are allowed to eat one M&M®, EXCEPT for the child that spilled them.
4. The teacher says to the child that spilled the M&M'S®, "Oh no! You spilled the M&M'S®. Are you going to get really mad and run away from your friends?" (Substitute with the individual child's negative behaviors). The child is prompted to say "No." The teacher responds, "Of course not, because it's just a game. Instead of getting mad, you can just be cool. You say, 'Be cool!'" Children are prompted to shrug their shoulders and say, "Be cool."
5. Repeat steps 3-4 with each child that spills the M&M'S®.

Reinforcers

Children are praised verbally, physically (high fives, tickles, hugs, pats on the back, sensory input), and with positive facial expressions for not engaging in negative behaviors during the game. All children are reinforced at the end of the game with primary reinforcers (M&M'S®) and secondary reinforcers (high fives, tickles) for being cool.

Week 5	Responds with Appropriate Affect in Frustrating Social Situations
Day 2	Tuesday — Gift Exchange

▪ Introduction to the Topic

"This week, we are learning to BE COOL. You guys did SUCH a great job yesterday being cool. Even when you spilled the M&M'S®, you all got some in the end because you all stayed cool." Continue to repeat the cues again. "When we feel mad, should we cry? No! We should stay cool and keep playing. We can stay cool by breathing, squeezing our hands, closing our eyes, keeping our body calm and still, and saying to ourselves, 'Be cool, it's just a game,' as many times as we need to. If we stay cool, good things will happen; but if we lose our cool, we will lose the game, lose the fun, and get nothing. Remember yesterday? Good things did happen—everyone got treats!"

Materials

- One really desirable item (e.g., cookies) wrapped in wrapping paper
- Miscellaneous items (e.g., Lego®, plastic spoon, empty tape ring, empty cookie wrappers) wrapped in wrapping paper

Model the Skill

The teacher tells the children, "We are playing a gift game! Each of you will get a number. The person who gets #1 goes first and picks a gift from my bag and opens it. If your classmate doesn't like the gift, should he cry? No! Should he scream? No! Because if he does, good things will not happen! Then the person who picked #2 can either 'steal' the first child's gift or pick a new gift from the bag." Please note, a teacher can repeat the rhetorical questions and the cues as often as they feel necessary to help prevent the students from losing their cool. This activity works well and can continue to be explained while the children are participating.

Guided Lesson

1. Children sit in a circle on the floor with the teacher.
2. Children pick numbers from a hat.
3. The first child chooses and opens a gift from the bag.
4. If it's one of the miscellaneous items, the teacher reminds the child about being cool using all the verbal cues. The child is praised lavishly if he/she remains cool.
5. The second child either chooses a gift from the bag or "steals"

Child 1's gift.

6. Again, the teacher reminds both children about being cool using all the verbal cues, especially if Child 1 got the cookies and Child 2 "stole" them. Child 1 and 2 are praised.

7. This continues based upon the order of the numbers. Child 3 can choose a gift or steal a gift. Each time, all children are reminded to be cool and are praised for acting appropriately.

Reinforcers

Children are praised verbally, physically (high fives, tickles, hugs, pats on the back, sensory input), and with positive facial expressions for not engaging in negative behaviors during the game. The child that has the cookies in the end should be HIGHLY encouraged to share. If the child refuses to share, the teacher should have another package and give even more to those who remained cool when they received undesirable items or had their favored item "stolen."

Week 5	**Responds with Appropriate Affect in Frustrating Social Situations**
Day 3	Wednesday — Un-Favorite Colors

Introduction to the Topic

Given that this is such a challenging week, we suggest that you remind the children about the prior days' successes before each lesson. "Remember everyone, this week we are learning to BE COOL. You guys did SUCH a great job on Monday and Tuesday being cool. Even when you spilled the M&M'S®, you all got some in the end because you all stayed cool. Even when you didn't get the item you wanted, you stayed cool and everyone got some cookies." Repeat the cues again: "When we feel mad, should we cry? No! We should stay cool and keep playing. We can stay cool by breathing, squeezing our hands, closing our eyes, keeping our body calm and still, and saying to ourselves, 'Be cool, it's just a game,' as many times as we need. If we stay cool, good things will happen; but if we lose our cool, we will lose the game, lose the fun, and get nothing. Remember yesterday? Good things did happen—everyone got treats!"

Materials

- Colored Chalk
- Black paper with an outline of something (e.g., a house)

Model the Skill

Teacher A asks Teacher B which color chalk he/she would like to use. Then, Teacher A gives Teacher B a color of chalk that is NOT that color. Teacher A asks the children, "Should Teacher B cry? Should Teacher B quit? NO! Tracher B should be cool." Again, use the verbal cues above in this context.

Guided Lesson

1. Children sit in a circle on the floor around the paper drawing.
2. The teacher asks each child which color he/she wants.
3. The teacher gives children a color that is NOT the one they asked for.
4. Once children have their colored chalk, they are instructed to color the picture.
5. The teacher then collects the chalk.
6. The teacher continues to ask children which color chalk they would like, sometimes giving the children what they asked for and sometimes giving them a different color.

7. At the end of the lesson, everyone who stayed cool gets to go hang the picture together in the yard and have free yard time. Explain that they are going to the yard instead of doing class work as a reward because they stayed cool and worked together. Any child that wasn't cool remains indoors and continues his/her class work.

Reinforcers

Children are praised verbally, physically (high fives, tickles, hugs, pats on the back, sensory input), and with positive facial expressions for not engaging in negative behaviors when they got a piece of chalk that was not their chosen color.

Week 5	**Responds with Appropriate Affect in Frustrating Social Situations**
Day 4	Thursday — Game Play

■ **Introduction to the Topic**

Again, we suggest you remind the children each day about the prior days' successes. "Remember everyone, this week we are learning to BE COOL. You guys did SUCH a great job all week being cool. Even when you spilled the M&M'S®, you all got some in the end because you stayed cool. Even when you didn't get the item you wanted, you stayed cool and everyone got cookies. Even when you didn't get the color chalk you wanted, you stayed cool and we all hung our picture and got yard time!" Repeat the cues again: "When we feel mad, should we cry? No! We should stay cool and keep playing. We can stay cool by breathing, squeezing our hands, closing our eyes, keeping our body calm and still, and saying to ourselves, 'Be cool, it's just a game,' as many times as we need. If we stay cool, good things will happen; but if we lose our cool, we will lose the game, lose the fun, and get nothing. Remember yesterday? Good things did happen—everyone got to play in the yard!"

Materials

- "Fun" game (e.g., Hullabaloo™)
- "Boring" game (e.g., 52 pickup)

Model the Skill

Teacher A plays a boring game while Teacher B plays a fun game. Teacher A demonstrates playing the boring game and staying cool. Teacher A states, "I want to play Hullabaloo™ but I'm going to stay cool and finish this game."

Guided Lesson

1. Children are divided into two groups.
2. Group 1 plays the "fun" game.
3. Group 2 plays the "boring" game. Group 2 should be highly reinforced for staying cool with all the cues and prompts.
4. After one round, one child from each group trades places. The child who moves from Group 1 ("fun" game) to Group 2 ("boring" game) needs strong cues and reinforcement. Group 2 should be continuously cued and reinforced to stay cool.
5. Continue to have the children trade places so that they all have a turn playing both of the games.

Reinforcers

Children are praised verbally, physically (high fives, tickles, hugs, pats on the back, sensory input), and with positive facial expressions for not engaging in negative behaviors while playing the "boring" game. Children are then all permitted to participate in another popular classroom game—or everyone can play Hullabaloo™ together!

Week 5	**Responds with Appropriate Affect in Frustrating Social Situations**
Day 5	Friday — "Be Cool" Olympics

Materials

- Two different-colored stickers
- Desirable prize (e.g., M&M'S®)
- Semi-undesirable prize (e.g., stickers)
- Undesirable prize (e.g., Legos®)
- Helmet or hat (used as the "special driver hat")
- Scooter for each team

Guided Lesson

■ Round 1

1. Children sit in a row, preferably in an outside playground area or if it must be done indoors, in the hallway.
2. Children are separated into two teams. The teams are distinguished by colors (e.g., yellow team and blue team). Children get a matching color sticker to help them remember what team they are on.
3. Children are assigned either the "driver" or "passenger" role. The importance of the driver is emphasized by giving him/her a "special driver hat."
4. Children are told, "Your team will get one of these prizes for winning." Hold up the different prizes: the desirable prize (e.g., M&M'S®) and the undesirable prize (e.g., one Lego®).
5. Children race by having the driver push a passenger on the scooter.
6. The winner receives the *undesirable* prize. Help the children stay cool with verbal cues. Ask them if they had fun racing and be sure to tell them there will be more chances to play and win.

■ Round 2

1. Children switch team colors.
2. Children switch roles. The driver becomes the passenger and the passenger becomes the driver.

3. Children race by having the driver push a passenger on the scooter.

4. The teacher stops the race in the middle and makes the children switch roles. This is done simply to make the race more interesting and give the children a chance to take turns being the driver/passenger. The teacher can blow a whistle and have everyone switch places, switch their stickers, or even switch teams. This can also be done to reinforce the goal of the lesson to a certain child or group of children that have a particularly hard time losing. Remember, this week is about developing the skills to respond appropriately to frustrating social situations. If a child really has a hard time losing, make sure to switch the race so that they do indeed lose, then prompt them to be cool.

5. Children may find losing the race disappointing enough so that prizes should not be distributed. If that is not the case, the winners can be presented with a semi-undesirable prize. Remind everyone to be cool, using all the strategies learned this week.

Reinforcers

This game is the last activity of the week. The higher-functioning children will assume that they will get the "desirable" item at the end of the activity regardless of whether they win or lose as long as they stay cool (because the previous activities were structured in this manner). As a result, DO NOT immediately give children the desirable item. Instead, present or discuss it during another time of the day and then reinforce them with the desirable item.

Week 5 | Responds with Appropriate Affect in Frustrating Social Situations
Generalization Ideas For The Classroom

Generalizing "Be Cool"

Remind children that although they may not get what they want in the following situations, they should still "be cool" (use the cues of breathing, squeezing hands, repeating the words, closing their eyes, etc.) as good things will come to them eventually.

- Classroom Jobs: Assign children their least favorite jobs for the day. Inform them that if they remain cool, they can pick their favorite job tomorrow.

- Snack Time: Withhold each child's favorite snack. Remind them that if they are cool, they can have their snack at the end of the day.

- In-Class Free Time: Pick one special helper who gets to pick the in-class free time activity (e.g., everyone plays with trains). Remind the other children that if they are cool, they can pick the next activity (either that day or the next).

- Recess: Pick one special helper to pick the activities that all children must engage in for the first few minutes of recess. Children cannot go to their favorite outdoor activity until they play with the chosen activity first. Remind them that if they stay cool, they can go to their favored activity next.

- Lunch: Provide children with a treat that comes in various colors (e.g., popsicles, M&M'S®). Hand out the item and try to give children a color or flavor that you know is not their favorite. Remind them that if they are cool, they will get a treat, even if it's not their favorite. If they are not cool, they won't get anything.

Books

- Dr. Seuss. *"The Zax" The Sneetches and Other Stories.* Random House, 1961.

- Katz, Karen. *No Hitting.* Grosset & Dunlap, 2004.

- Verdick, Elizabeth. *Feet Are Not for Kicking.* Illus. Marieka Heinlen. Free Spirit Publishing, Inc., 2004.

- Agassi, Martine. *Hands Are Not for Hitting.* Illus. Marieka Heinlen. Free Spirit Publishing, Inc., 2002.

- Harker, Jillian. *Don't Give Up Duck.* Parragon Inc., 2008.

- Casalis, Anna. *Tip the Mouse Doesn't Want to Go to Nursery School.* Illus. Marco Campanella. Sandy Creek, 2008.

- Mayer, Mercer. *I Was So Mad.* Random House Books for Young Readers, 2000.

- Viorst, Judith. *Alexander and the Terrible, Horrible, No Good, Very Bad Day.* Illus. Ray Cruz. Atheneum, 2009.

- Demas, Corinne. *Always in Trouble.* Illus. Noah Z. Jones. Scholastic Press, 2009.

- Bang, Molly. *When Sophie Gets Angry - Really, Really Angry.* Blue Sky Press, 1999.

- Crary, Elizabeth, and Shari Steelsmith. *When You're Mad and You Know It.* Illus. Mits Katayama. Parenting Press, 1996.

- Yolen, Jane, and Mark Teague. *How Do Dinosaurs Say Goodnight?* Blue Sky Press, 2000.

Week 6 | Accepts Differences in Routines Appropriately
"Sometimes Things are Different"

Behavioral Objective

Children will learn to respond appropriately to not getting their way, to disruptions in routines, or to violations of the rules.

Identify the Skill Components

- Language
- Cognitive understanding of "same" and "different"
- Recall skills (limited memory required)

Lessons and Materials for the Week

Day	Lesson	Materials
Monday	Memory Match	Any memory game or cards that match
Tuesday	Oreo Cookie Game	Oreo Matchin' Middles™ Game
Wednesday	Dress-Up	Variety of dress-up clothing, including accessories
Thursday	S'Match!™	S'Match!™ Game
Friday	Jelly Bean Roll	Jelly beans, tape, opaque long paper towel rolls, PVC pipes or any material that makes a tube, or a marble run toy that is commercially available

For the Parents

Dear Parents,

This week, our social skill classroom behavior is:

Category 3: Turn Taking and Simple Social Play	
Week 6	Accepts Differences in Routines Appropriately "Sometimes Things are Different"

Children seek out routines and consistency in their environment. Although this is an important developmental skill, some children take this need too far by getting extremely upset when something is different than what they expect. The ability to accept that things can be different than what is expected is an important skill not only in the classroom (where unexpected things constantly occur) but in the home and community as well. We live in a fluid and changing world.

This week, we're teaching children that sometimes things are different. When they expect something, or even demand that something remain the same, they should not get upset because it changes. Keep in mind that children don't necessarily require a good reason or explanation to understand that things are different. Instead, they can understand that differences and changes in routine exist and happen. Children can shrug their shoulders and simply say, "Oh, sometimes things are different!" and move on.

Please encourage your child to use the phrase, "Sometimes things are different," in situations where they expect sameness or in routine situations. You know your child's routines and expectations. You can watch your child and see them anticipate certain activities and as he/she looks for that routine, you can model the skill by saying, "Oh, _____ is different; sometimes things are different." Encourage your child to repeat the phrase consistently. You can also prompt by simply using the initial part of the phrase, "Oh, sometimes things are _____," and have your child fill in the word "different." You can then follow-up with last week's catch phrase, "Remember, 'be cool' and good things will happen!"

In each of the following situations, preempt the change with the verbal cue, "Remember, sometimes things are _____," or model the full sentence.

Here are some ways to practice this skill at home:

- At dinner, sit in your child's regular seat and as they walk towards the table, model the language, "I'm sitting in this seat tonight. Remember, sometimes things are _____." Praise and reward your child by letting them know that if/when they are cool, a dessert may follow dinner.

- When going to the store, if you always buy something for your child or if they always ride in a cart, let them know that during this trip, there will not be any special treats or riding in the cart. Remind him/her that sometimes things are different and to be cool – he/she will certainly get something the next time you go to the store. In this situation, please keep your shopping trip extremely short – get in and out quickly and heavily praise your child for doing something different and being cool.

- There are numerous examples of children's resistance to change that we have encountered from families (always having to put the key in the door, always having to park cars in a certain way, always needing to wear a certain shirt, never tolerating an item of clothing that has dirt on it, always wanting to have a particular plate/bowl/cup, always needing to go before a sibling to get in a car, etc.). The catch phrase, "Remember, sometimes things are different!" can be applied in all of these situations.

Week 6	Accepts Differences in Routines Appropriately
Day 1	Monday — Memory Match

■ Introduction to the Topic

"This week, we are learning about same and different. Sometimes, things are the same and sometimes things are different. When things are different, sometimes that makes us feel mad. But even if things are different, we have to stay cool. When we stay cool, good things happen!"

Materials

- Any memory game or cards that match

Model the Skill

Teacher A turns over two cards and shows them to Teacher B. If they are a match, Teacher A says, "They are the same!" or if they are not a match, "They are different!"

Guided Lesson

Children sit in a circle on the floor with the memory game in the middle. The cards are set up in rows. Lay out the appropriate number of cards to match the memory skills of your children; the goal is for children to be able to remember where the matches are.

■ Round 1

1. One child is selected to go first.
2. The child turns over two cards.
3. The teacher asks, "Is it the same or different?"
4. The child is prompted to answer correctly (Note: Do not allow your children to make too many errors correctly determining if they are same or different to ensure that they learn the appropriate skill).
5. If the cards are the same, then he/she gets to keep the pair. If the tiles are not the same, he/she puts the cards back in their original place and is prompted to say, "Oh, sometimes things are different!" and then it is the next child's turn.

■ Round 2

1. Use the same procedures as Round 1 but in this round, mix the place-ment of the cards after each turn to encourage mismatches.

2. When children choose cards that aren't a match, have them use the catch phrase, "It's different!"

Reinforcers

Children are praised verbally, physically (high fives, tickles, hugs, pats on the back, sensory input), and with positive facial expressions for correctly identi-fying same and different. Children can also show their matches at the end of the game to the teacher and to their friends for additional reinforcement.

Week 6	**Accepts Differences in Routines Appropriately**
Day 2	Tuesday – Oreo Cookie Game

Materials

- Oreo Matchin' Middles™ game

Model the Skill

Teacher A has one side of the Oreo cookie and grabs another side out of the cookie jar. If it is a match, Teacher A says, "It's the same!" and if it is not a match, "It's different."

Guided Lesson

1. Children sit in a circle on the floor. The teacher hands out the black side of several cookies to each child. Encourage the children to examine the shapes on the cookie.

2. On each turn, the child puts his/her hand into the cookie jar and pulls out the white side of the cookie.

3. If it is a match, the child is prompted to say, "It's the same!" and then put the two sides together.

4. If it is not a match, the child is prompted to say, "Oh, sometimes things are different!" and then put the white side of the cookie back into the jar.

5. Repeat so that all children get at least one turn.

Reinforcers

Children are praised verbally, physically (high fives, tickles, hugs, pats on the back, sensory input), and with positive facial expressions for correctly identifying same and different. Children can also pretend to munch on the cookies and laugh together at the end of the activity.

Week 6 Accepts Differences in Routines Appropriately
Day 3 Wednesday – Dress-Up

Materials

- Variety of dress-up clothes including accessories

Model the Skill

Teacher A stands in front of the group and prompts the children to examine what he/she is wearing and then goes out of the room and puts on one new article of clothing. Teacher A comes back inside and asks, "What's different?" Teacher B correctly identifies the new piece of clothing that has been added.

Guided Lesson

1. Children sit in a circle on the floor.
2. One child is selected to be the "model."
3. The child stands in front of the group and allows the children to look at and comment on what he/she is wearing.
4. The child then leaves the room with one teacher.
5. Once outside, the child puts on one new piece of clothing.
6. The child comes back in, stands in front of the group and asks, "What's different?"
7. Children are called upon to guess what is different about the model child's outfit.
8. Repeat so that all children get at least one turn being the model and each child has a turn to correctly identify what is different.

Reinforcers

Children are praised verbally, physically (high fives, tickles, hugs, pats on the back, sensory input), and with positive facial expressions for correctly identifying what is different about the model's clothes. In addition, the model can be chosen based on the child that correctly identifies the item that is different.

Week 6	**Accepts Differences in Routines Appropriately**
Day 4	Thursday – S'Match!™ Game

Materials

- S'Match!™ Game

Model the Skill

Teacher A spins the spinner to find out what needs to match (i.e., category, number or color). Then he/she turns over two tiles and if they are a match says, "They are the same (category, number, color)!"

Guided Lesson

1. Children sit in a circle on the floor.

2. One child is chosen by the teacher to go first.

3. The spinner is passed to the child who uses it to determine if he/she is looking for a match based on category, number, or color.

4. The child then turns over two cards and determines if they are a match based upon the descriptor.

5. If it is a match, the child is prompted to say, "They are the same (category, number, color)!"

6. If it is not a match, the child is prompted to say, "Oh, sometimes things are different!" and then the child returns the cards and passes the spinner to the next child.

7. Continue playing until each child has a turn to find a match.

Reinforcers

Children are praised verbally, physically (high fives, tickles, hugs, pats on the back, sensory input), and with positive facial expressions for correctly identifying same and different. Children can show their matches to teachers and friends at the end for additional reinforcement.

Week 6 Accepts Differences in Routines Appropriately
Day 5 Friday – Jelly Bean Roll

Materials

- Jelly beans
- Opaque long paper towel rolls, PVC pipes or any material that makes a tube, or a marble run toy that is commercially available
- Tape

Model the Skill

Teacher A and Teacher B take turns putting down one piece of the track for the marble roll together. (Do not spend a great deal of time building a complex track – two connected pieces is sufficient). Teacher A gives Teacher B a jelly bean and says, "Close your eyes. I will pick a color jelly bean and send it to you secretly. See if it matches yours!" Teacher A picks a different color jelly bean and holds it at the top of the pipe. Teacher A says, "Open your eyes!" and simultaneously drops the jelly bean down the track. When the jelly bean comes out at the bottom, Teacher B says, "It's a different color! I have to give it back to you," and gives it back to Teacher A. Teacher A says, "Let's try again," and repeats the bean drop, this time with a matching color. Teacher B says, "It is the same!" and then eats them both!

Guided Lesson

1. Children sit in a row. Each child is given a piece of tubing to build the track. If using the paper towel rolls, tape them together. The end track is handed to the teacher. This step can be skipped if the teacher wants to provide a readymade track.

2. The teacher hands out different color jelly beans to the children.

3. The teacher says, "Should we eat our jelly bean now?"

4. Children are prompted to say, "No!"

5. The teacher says, "Do not eat your jelly bean yet. Wait until you see what color jelly bean comes out of the tube. If the jelly bean is the same color as yours, when I point to you, say 'Same!' If the jelly bean is a different color, when I point to you, say 'Different!' If your jelly bean is the same color, you get to eat both!"

6. The teacher says, "Remember, do not say 'same' or 'different' until I point to you."

7. The teacher says, "Close your eyes!"

8. The teacher chooses a jelly bean and holds it at the entrance of the tube so none of the children can see the color. One end of the tube is held high so that the bean falls out of the bottom.

9. The teacher says, "Open your eyes!"

10. The teacher then drops the bean into the tube. When it comes out of the bottom, the teacher points to each child and asks, "Same or different?"

11. If the jelly bean is a different color, the child is prompted to say, "Oh, it's a different color... sometimes things are different!" If the jelly bean is the same color, the teacher gives the matching bean to the child who should correctly identify it as the same. The child is permitted to eat both jelly beans.

12. Repeat steps 3-11 so that each child eventually gets a matching jelly bean and a chance to eat them.

Reinforcers

Children are praised verbally, physically (high fives, tickles, hugs, pats on the back, sensory input), and with positive facial expressions for correctly identifying same and different on each turn. Children are also naturally reinforced when they get to eat the jelly beans.

Week 6 Accepts Differences in Routines Appropriately
Generalization Ideas For The Classroom

Generalizing "Sometimes Things are Different"

Remind children that last week, they worked on "being cool" in situations where they didn't get what they wanted. This week, remind them that although sometimes things don't go the way that they want them to, they can still "stay cool" because "sometimes things are different." Good things may happen when things are the same and good things may happen when things are different too!

- Lining Up: Surprise children by having them line up at a different location and when they do, have a fun activity waiting for them.

- Mats: Have children pick a mat to sit on (e.g., circle time mats) and after they pick them and sit down, have them stand up and sit on the back side of them. Place a fun sticker on the backs so that they receive a reward for sitting on the mats differently. Remind them, "Sometimes things are different!"

- Backwards Day: Flip the daily schedule around. Do what you usually do at the end of the day first and go through the day backwards. After each activity, point to the schedule, act surprised and say, "We are doing lunch before snack! Wow! Sometimes things are different but it is fun!"

- Sit on the Floor vs. Sit on a Chair: Switch up children's routines (e.g., if children always sit on chairs for circle time, have them sit on the floor and vice versa).

- Examine Individual Routines: Look carefully at the routines of the children in your class. For example, some children always play on the yard in a certain order (e.g., bikes first). Remove their preferred option and tell them, "Today, you will do the jungle gym first. Remember, sometimes things are different."

Books

- Abel, Simone. *Color Match Board Book*. Penguin Putnam, 1999.

- Barth, April. *Same Size, Same Shape*. Newmark Learning, 2010.

- Hayward, Linda and Cathy Goldsmith. *Sneetches are Sneetches: Learn about Same and Different (A Dr. Seuss Beginner Fun Book)*. Random House, 1995.

- Kates, Bobby and Joe Mathieu. *We're Different, We're the Same (Sesame Street)*. Random House, 1992.

- Kalman, Bobbie. *Is it the Same or Different?* Crabtree Publishing Company, 2008.

- McCarthy, Rebecca. *Monster Match: A Memory Book*. Running Press Miniature Editions, 2009.

- Vietro, Lee. *Memory Match Game Books*. Innovative Kids, 2003.

NOTE:

There are many activity workbooks that focus on the concept of Same vs. Different. These can be used to "read" or to carry out, generalize, and facilitate learning.

Week 7	**Responds with Appropriate Affect in Positive Social Situations**
	"Feel Alright"

Behavioral Objective

Children will learn to respond with appropriate affect in a positive social situation.

Identify the Skill Components

- Language: verbalizing "Alright"
- Ability to feel happy or excited
- Ability to control self-stimulatory behaviors

Lessons and Materials for the Week

Day	Lesson	Materials
Monday	Scooter Race	Scooter, party streamers
Tuesday	Singing Show	Puppet show display
Wednesday	Where's Freddy?	Three paper cups, "Freddy" the toy frog
Thursday	Whac-a-Mole™ game	Whac-a-Mole™ game, construction hats
Friday	Pop-Out Teacher!	Divider with three curtained stations

For the Parents

Dear Parents,

This week, our social skill classroom behavior is:

Category 3: Turn Taking and Simple Social Play	
Week 7	Responds with Appropriate Affect in Positive Social Situations "Feel Alright"

Some children do not know how to respond appropriately when they are really excited or happy. Some children may yell inappropriately, jump, run around, or flap their hands. It is important for us to teach children to have appropriate affect in positive social situations.

Please encourage your child to use the catch phrase, "Alright!" and swing one arm when faced with positive social situations to help him/her to express excitement in an appropriate way.

Be sure to incorporate saying, "Alright!" while swinging one arm in each of the following situations.

Here are some ways to practice this skill at home:
• Serve your child a favorite food for dinner.
• Allow your child to stay awake for an extra 10 minutes.
• Read your child an extra bedtime story.
• Let your child pick what dessert he/she will have.
• Arrange for a play date with your child's best friend.

Week 7	**Responds with Appropriate Affect in Positive Social Situations**
Day 1	Monday — Scooter Race

■ Introduction to the Topic

"This week, we are going to learn how to show friends that we feel alright!"

Materials

- Scooter
- Party streamers

Model the Skill

The teacher models the skill by using a scooter to race to the finish line, which is made of party streamers. When the teacher gets to the finish line, he/she breaks through the party streamers. All of the teachers cheer. The teacher expresses his/her excitement by saying, "Alright!" and swinging one arm.

Guided Lesson

1. Children sit on a bench in the playground or at the end of the hallway if indoors.
2. Two teachers stand across from them holding a finish line made of streamers.
3. Children take turns using a scooter to race down to the finish line.
4. When children get to the finish line, they break through the party streamers.
5. All of the other children are prompted to cheer for their peer while he/she is racing.
6. After the children break through the finish line, they are prompted to express their excitement by saying, "Alright!" and shaking/swinging one arm up in the air.
7. Repeat with each child.

Reinforcers

At the end, all of the children run together to the finish line and break through the party streamers. Children are reinforced with verbal praise, physical praise (high fives, tickles, hugs, pats on the back, sensory input), tangibles (stickers), and positive facial expressions for doing a great job "feeling alright."

Week 7 | Responds with Appropriate Affect in Positive Social Situations
Day 2 | Tuesday — Singing Show

Materials

- Puppet Theater

Model the Skill

The teacher models the skill by singing his/her favorite song. All of the teachers cheer. The teacher expresses his/her excitement by saying, "Alright!" and swinging one arm.

Guided Lesson

1. Children sit in a row on chairs.
2. Children take turns singing their favorite song to their peers in front of the puppet theater.
3. All of the other children are prompted to cheer for their peer.
4. When their song is finished, children express their excitement over a job well done by saying, "Alright!" and swinging one arm.

Reinforcers

Children are reinforced with verbal praise, physical praise (high fives, tickles, hugs, pats on the back, sensory input), tangibles (stickers), and positive facial expressions for doing a great job "feeling alright."

Week 7	Responds with Appropriate Affect in Positive Social Situations
Day 3	Wednesday — Where's Freddy?

Materials

- Three paper cups
- "Freddy" the toy frog

Model the Skill

The teacher models the skill by picking up one of three paper cups to see if Freddy is under it. When the teacher sucessfully finds Freddy, he/she expresses excitement by saying, "Alright!" and swinging one arm.

Guided Lesson

1. Children sit in a row on the floor.
2. The teacher sits in front of the children at a table.
3. The teacher places three upside-down paper cups on the table.
4. The teacher says, "I have three cups. Two of these cups are empty. The third cup has Freddy under it."
5. Children take turns guessing which cup is hiding Freddy.
6. When children are successful in finding Freddy, all of the other children are prompted to cheer.
7. When they find Freddy, children express their excitement by saying, "Alright!" and swinging one arm.
8. If the children are unsuccessful at finding Freddy, the teacher says, "It's okay. Try again next time! You'll have another chance."
9. The teacher mixes up which cup Freddy is under after each turn.
10. Repeat so that each child has a chance to guess where the toy frog is hidden.

Reinforcers

Children are reinforced with verbal praise, physical praise (high fives, tickles, hugs, pats on the back, sensory input), tangibles (stickers), and positive facial expressions for doing a great job "feeling alright."

Week 7 Responds with Appropriate Affect in Positive Social Situations
Day 4 Thursday — Whac-a-Mole™ Game

Materials

- Whac-a-Mole™ board game
- Dress-up construction hats to match the color of Whac-a-Mole construction hats

Model the Skill

The teacher models how to play Whac-a-Mole by hitting the mole with the hammer when its construction hat lights up. The teacher expresses his/her excitement when successful by saying, "Alright!" and swinging one arm.

Guided Lesson

1. Children sit in a circle on the floor.
2. The teacher gives each child a construction hat that matches the color of a Whac-a-Mole's construction hat.
3. Children hit their respective Whac-a-Mole when its construction hat lights up.
4. With each successful hit, children express their excitement by saying, "Alright!" and swinging one arm.

Reinforcers

Children are reinforced with verbal praise, physical praise (high fives, tickles, hugs, pats on the back, sensory input), tangibles (stickers), and positive facial expressions for doing a great job "feeling alright."

Week 7	**Responds with Appropriate Affect in Positive Social Situations**
Day 5	Friday — Pop-Out Teacher!

Materials

- Divider with three curtained sections

Model the Skill

Teacher A hides behind one of the "doors" of the divider. Teacher B models the skill by picking one of the three sections of the divider and checking to see if Teacher A is hiding behind it. Teacher B picks the correct door and expresses his/her excitement when Teacher A pops out by saying, "Alright!" and swinging one arm.

Guided Lesson

1. Children sit in a row on chairs.
2. Teacher A places the three-curtained divider in front of children.
3. Teacher A labels the three sections of the divider: Door #1, Door #2, and Door #3.
4. Children take turns picking a door to see if Teacher B is hiding behind it.
5. Teacher B jumps out at the child if he/she is successful.
6. All of the other children are prompted to cheer for their peer.
7. If a child picks the right curtain and Teacher B pops out, all of the children express their excitement by saying, "Alright!" and swinging one arm.

Reinforcers

Children are reinforced with verbal praise, physical praise (high fives, tickles, hugs, pats on the back, sensory input), tangibles (stickers), and positive facial expressions for doing a great job "feeling alright."

Week 7 | Responds with Appropriate Affect in Positive Social Situations
Generalization Ideas For The Classroom

Generalizing "Feeing Alright"

Anytime you give children something that makes them happy, encourage them to verbalize "Alright!" with an arm gesture. Some examples are: when you assign a child his/her favorite job to do, when you give a group of children free time, when you give children access to special toys, or when you give children access to their favorite art materials.

- Lunch: Ask parents to pack their child's favorite lunch. Encourage children to say, "Alright!" and swing one arm when they open their lunch or get their favorite snack.

- Stickers: Randomly pass out stickers throughout the day. Encourage children to say, "Alright!" and swing one arm when they get a sticker.

Books

- Ormerod, Jan, and Lindsay Gardiner. *If You're Happy and You Know It!* Star Bright Books, 2003.

- Cummings, Carol. *Sticks and Stones.* Teaching Inc., 1992.

- Rey, Margaret, and H.A. Rey. *Curious George at the Beach.* Houghton Mifflin, 1999.

- Alborough, Jez. *Some Dogs Do.* Candlewick, 2003.

Week 8 | Takes Turns on Playground Equipment
"Playground Time"

Behavioral Objective

Children will learn how to take turns on playground/classroom equipment by allowing others to go ahead of them.

Identify the Skill Components

- Language: telling peers it's their turn
- Ability to follow directions from a peer
- Cognitive capacity to understand that people take turns during activities/games
- Ability to take turns
- Ability to allow another child to go first
- Allows another child to choose the activity
- Possesses strategies for managing play with others on the playground

Lessons and Materials for the Week

Day	Lesson	Materials
Monday	The 10 Count	Swings, spinner, see-saw, jump rope, drinking fountain
Tuesday	Slide Patterns	Slide, stickers, sticker pattern
Wednesday	Ball Games	Basketballs, hoops
Thursday	Obstacle Course	Playground equipment, jump ropes, hula hoops, balls
Friday	Bike Relay	Bikes, chalk

For the Parents

Dear Parents,

This week, our social skill classroom behavior is:

Category 3: Turn Taking and Simple Social Play	
Week 8	Takes Turns on Playground Equipment "Playground Time"

Many children have trouble taking turns with common items on the playground or in the classroom. You can help teach your child this skill by encouraging him/her to share common items in the home.

Please encourage your child to use the words "My turn/Your turn" when they encounter toys or equipment that are commonly owned. This means children cannot not claim it as their own but instead must take turns. This is extremely relevant at the park with equipment like swings and slides which must be appropriately shared with other children.

Here are some ways to practice this skill at home:
• At the park, encourage your child to take turns on the swing and slide using the words, "My turn/Your turn."
• Take sand equipment but limit the amount. Take only one bucket, one shovel, and one rake to the park. Have your child find one peer to take turns using the sand toys with.
• If your child has a sibling, encourage both children to take turns picking which shows or movies they will watch.
• During bedtime, take turns picking which stories you will read (if a sibling is available, have the children take turns picking).
• If a sibling is available, provide one bowl of snacks/food and have the children take turns getting a few at a time.

Week 8 | Takes Turns on Playground Equipment
Day 1 | Monday — The 10 Count

■ Introduction to the Topic

"This week, we are going to practice taking turns with our friends on the playground."

Materials

- Swings
- Spinner (or small carousel)
- See-saw
- Jump rope
- Drinking fountain

Model the Skill

Teacher A says to Teacher B, "Your turn," and allows Teacher B to use the target playground equipment. Teacher A counts to 10 and then says, "My turn." Teacher B stops the activity, gives the equipment to Teacher A, and says, "Your turn."

Guided Lesson

1. Children sit in a line on the playground facing the equipment.
2. Two children are selected to demonstrate sharing.
3. One child allows the other child to go first by saying, "Your turn," and counts to 10 while the peer uses the equipment.
4. After the count of 10, the child who was counting says, "My turn!"
5. The child who was playing must give the equipment to the peer by saying, "Your turn."
6. Repeat steps 2-5 using different pairs of children and different playground equipment.

Indoor Option

Playground equipment may be substituted with different center activities in the classroom.

Reinforcers

Children are praised verbally, physically (high fives, tickles), and with positive facial expressions for allowing their peers to have a turn. No need for tangibles as they are on the playground!

| Week 8 | Takes Turns on Playground Equipment |
| Day 2 | Tuesday — Slide Patterns |

Materials

- Slide
- Stickers (can be different stickers or different colors of the same sticker)
- Sticker pattern (see below in "Set Up")

Set Up

Place a row of stickers in a pattern on paper (e.g., red dot, green dot, blue dot, yellow dot). This establishes the order in which the children will go down the slide as each child receives a corresponding color sticker.

Model the Skill

Teacher A and Teacher B show the children that they have a sticker on their hands (red dot for Teacher A and green dot for Teacher B). Teacher A says, "This pattern (point to the paper) tells me that the red dot sticker goes first. I have a red dot sticker, so it's my turn to go first." Teacher B says, "This pattern (point to the paper) tells me that the green dot sticker goes second. I have a green dot sticker, so it's my turn to go second after Teacher A." Each teacher places their sticker on the pattern before they go down the slide.

Guided Lesson

1. Children sit in a row in front of the teacher by the slide.
2. The teacher passes out stickers to each child. Then the teacher shows the children the sticker pattern and re-explains the rules. The rules are:
    a. Everyone gets a turn to go down the slide.
    b. The order to go down the slide depends on the sticker pattern.
    c. The child that has a sticker that matches the first sticker goes first.
    d. The child that has a sticker that matches the second sticker goes next, and so forth.
3. Children should monitor whose turn is next based on the sticker pattern.
4. When it is their turn, children put their stickers on the pattern and go down the slide.
5. Children are encouraged to use the words, "It's my turn next" or, "It's your turn now."

Indoor Option

Slide may be substituted with riding a scooter from one end of the room to the other, taking turns based on the sticker pattern.

Reinforcers

Children are praised verbally, physically (high fives, tickles), and with positive facial expressions for taking turns and allowing their peers to have a turn. No need for tangibles as they are on the playground!

Week 8 Takes Turns on Playground Equipment
Day 3 Wednesday — Ball Games

Materials

- Basketballs
- Hoop

■ Round 1

Model the Skill

Teacher A passes a ball to Teacher B while calling Teacher B's name, saying, "Here ___."

Guided Lesson

1. Divide all the children into two groups and have them line up and face each other. The children facing each other will be partners.
2. One child starts with the ball.
3. The child passes the ball to his/her partner using a bounce pass while calling out the peer by name, saying, "Here ___."
4. The partner passes the ball back to the original child using the same type of pass.
5. Try this drill with other types of passes including: Chest pass, Overhead pass, Roll pass.
6. During each exchange, the children are prompted to call out their partners' names before they pass the ball saying, "Here ___."

■ Round 2

Model the Skill

Teacher A passes a ball to Teacher B while calling Teacher B's name. Teacher B shoots the ball into the hoop and both teachers cheer.

Guided Lesson

1. Divide all the children into two groups. Have one group line up about 10 feet away from the hoop—this will be the "Passing Line." The other group lines up next to the hoop—this will be the "Shooting Line."

2. The first children in each line are partners.

3. The child in the Passing Line starts with the ball and passes it to the child in the Shooting Line while calling the child's name.

4. The child in the Shooting Line catches the ball and shoots a basket.

5. Both children are prompted to cheer whether or not the ball goes in the basket.

6. Children switch roles, pass and shoot, then go to the back of each line.

Indoor Option

Use a small ball instead of a basketball and use a bucket instead of a basketball hoop. Also, instead of overhead passes and large motor movements, have the children do more contained passing (tossing, rolling, handing the balls).

Reinforcers

Children in the Passing Line are praised verbally, physically (high fives, tickles), and with positive facial expressions for allowing their peers to have a turn. No need for tangibles as they are on the playground! The praise should be focused on the "assisting" child who did not get to shoot the basket. Emphasize praising this child for passing to their peer.

Week 8 Takes Turns on Playground Equipment
Day 4 Thursday — Obstacle Course

Materials

- Playground equipment (slides, swings)
- Jump ropes
- Hula hoops
- Balls

Model the Skill

Teachers leave jump ropes, hula hoops, and balls around the playground. Teacher A demonstrates 3-4 activities (e.g., going down the slide, jumping rope three times, tossing a ball at the wall, and running under the swing). Teacher B then imitates the activities.

Guided Lesson

1. Children sit in a row facing the playground equipment.
2. One child is selected to go and complete a 3- to 4-step sequence of his/her choosing using the available equipment. The teacher should define, "Please go and pick 4 things to do and your classmates will follow you!"
3. The leader can be verbally, physically, or gesturally prompted to pick the first activity (e.g., if the child is not picking something, the teacher can help them select the swing first). If the child needs more assistance, prompt and guide them through each of the activities.
4. All of the other children are prompted to follow the leader through the obstacle course.
5. When everyone finishes that course, another leader is selected and prompted to pick his/her own activities.

Indoor Option

Playground activity options may be substituted with indoor activities. A hula hoop, soft balls, a balance beam, cones, etc. can be used.

Reinforcers

Children are praised verbally, physically (high fives, tickles), and with positive facial expressions for allowing their peers to have a turn. No need for tangibles as they are on the playground!

Week 8	**Takes Turns on Playground Equipment**
Day 5	Friday — Bike Relay

Materials

- Bikes
- Chalk

Set Up

Teacher draws a short path with the chalk and a line for the children to sit behind.

Model the Skill

Teacher A races Teacher B to the bike. When Teacher A wins she says, "You go first," and allows Teacher B to ride the bike around the path first.

Guided Lesson

1. Children sit in a row behind the chalk line.
2. Four children are selected to race to the bike.
3. The winner of the race is the "Chooser."
4. The Chooser gets to pick the order of who gets to ride the bike by saying, "You go first."
5. When the other children have had a turn, the "Chooser" gets to ride the bike.
6. Repeat steps 2-5 until all the children have a turn racing to the bike and riding it.

Indoor Option

Chalk may be substituted with masking tape on the floor. Bikes may be substituted with scooters.

Reinforcers

Children are praised verbally, physically (high fives, tickles), and with positive facial expressions for allowing their peers to have a turn. No need for tangibles as they are on the playground!

Week 8 Takes Turns on Playground Equipment
Generalization Ideas For The Classroom

Generalizing "Playground Time"

- Recess: Pick one activity (e.g., bikes, swing) that all children must take turns engaging in for the first five minutes of recess.

- Recess Buddies: Pair children up into recess buddies. Have each pair pick an activity that they will take turns doing.

- Free Play: Pick one activity (e.g., dollhouse, cars, pretend food) that all children must take turns engaging in.

- Art Buddies: Pair children up and give each pair one set of materials (e.g., scissors, glue) and encourage children to allow their peers to go first.

- Calendar or any teacher-led group: Call children up in pairs and have them take turns doing the activity required (or have one help the other by passing materials). For example, if you are using a felt board and are asking a child to come up and place items on it, call up two children, have one hold all the felt pieces and have the other request the felt pieces one at a time.

Books

- Murphy, Stuart J. *Just Enough Carrots.* Illus. Frank Remkiewicz. HarperCollins, 1997.

- Murphy, Stuart J. *Game Time!* Illus. Cynthia Jabar. HarperCollins, 2000.

- Sturges, Philemon. *I Love School!* Illus. Shari Halpern. HarperCollins, 2006.

Category 4 | Cooperation

- **Week 1**   **Helps to Complete an Activity That Has Already Been Started (54 months)**
  Children will learn to complete an activity that has been started.

- **Week 2**   **Goes Along With an Idea or Action of Peers (60 months)**
  Children will learn to go along with a peer's action or idea.

- **Week 3**   **Listens Without Interrupting While Another Talks (72 months)**
  Children will learn not to interrupt teachers and peers.

Week 1	**Helps Complete an Activity That Has Been Started**
	"I Helped You Finish!"

Behavioral Objective

Children will learn to complete an activity that has been started by others.

Identify the Skill Components

- Ability to move on to another activity when prompted
- Ability to give up one's own activity when prompted
- Ability to finish someone else's project
- Ability to regulate emotions

Lessons and Materials for the Week

Day	Lesson	Materials
Monday	Drawing	Paper, crayons
Tuesday	Story Time	Picture cards
Wednesday	Poster Day	Butcher paper with block letters, markers, art supplies, glue
Thursday	Five Stations	Legos®, play dough, butcher paper, markers, craft (e.g., a picture frame with popsicle sticks), stringing beads, bell
Friday	Puzzle Switch	One puzzle per child, bell

For the Parents

Dear Parents,

This week, our social skill classroom behavior is:

Category 4: Cooperation	
Week 1	Helps to Complete an Activity That Has Already Been Started "I Helped You Finish! "

Many children move frequently between activities or leave a project before it is completed. Children also often have difficulty working on or adding to someone else's ideas.

Please encourage children to finish their work. Also, encourage your child to complete things for other people in the family and use the catch phrase, "I helped you finish!" You can model these skills daily by showing your child how you stay with a task until completion, as well as helping others with a task that has already been started.

Here are some ways to practice this skill at home:
• Start clearing the table and ask your child to finish the task for you. Any clean-up activity can be used in this manner.
• During any play situation, build a structure alongside your child and ask him/her to switch and finish each other's structures.
• Pick a familiar book and read the first part; then have the child finish reading the end of the book. If the child cannot read, they can describe it through the pictures.

Week 1	**Helps Complete an Activity That Has Been Started**
Day 1	Monday — Drawing

◼ Introduction to the Topic

"This week, we are going to practice finishing projects, activities, and work."

Materials

- Paper
- Crayons

Model the Skill

Teacher A models the skill by drawing a picture and then giving it to Teacher B to finish.

Guided Lesson

1. Children sit in a circle at the table.
2. The teacher passes out a paper and crayon to each child.
3. Each child draws a picture of a house.
4. Children trade drawings with a peer.
5. Children finish their peers' drawing.
6. Children return their peers' drawing and state, "I helped you finish your drawing!"

Reinforcers

Children are reinforced with verbal praise, physical praise (high fives, tickles, hugs, pats on the back, sensory input), tangibles (the pictures they drew), and positive facial expressions for finishing each other's pictures.

Week 1 | Helps Complete an Activity That Has Been Started
Day 2 | Tuesday — Story Time

Materials

- Picture Cards

Model the Skill

Teacher A models the skill by telling a story about a picture card. Teacher B adds to or finishes the story with his/her picture card. For example: Teacher A has a picture card of a girl having ice cream. Teacher A can say, "My name is Anna and I love chocolate ice cream." Teacher B has a picture card of a boy on a skateboard. Teacher B can say, "Oh no Anna, I'm going to crash into you!"

Guided Lesson

1. Children sit in a circle on the floor.

2. The teacher passes out picture cards to each child.

3. Teacher A puts a picture card in the center of the circle and begins a simple story (one or two sentences) related to the picture.

4. The next child puts a picture card next to the teacher's and says something simple about the card that should loosely relate to the teacher's picture card (if it doesn't relate, it's okay).

5. This continues until all the children have placed their cards down and related a simple story. In larger groups, break the children into groups of 3-4.

6. The teacher recites the completed story to the children at the end and states, "You helped me finish my story!"

7. The teacher queries the children: "What did you help me do?" The children are prompted to say, "I helped you finish the story!"

Reinforcers

Children are reinforced with verbal praise, physical praise (high fives, tickles, hugs, pats on the back, sensory input), tangibles (stickers), and positive facial expressions for helping to finish the teacher's story.

Week 1	**Helps Complete an Activity That Has Been Started**
Day 3	Wednesday — Poster Day

Materials

- Paper with a large block letter (you can match the letters to the children's names)
- Markers
- Art supplies
- Glue

Model the Skill

Teacher A models the skill by decorating his/her letter on the poster. Teacher B is simultaneously decorating his/her own letter. One of the teachers calls, "Switch" and they switch papers and finish decorating the other teacher's letter.

Guided Lesson

1. Children sit in a circle on the floor.
2. The teacher hands out a letter to each child.
3. Each child decorates one letter.
4. Upon the teacher's call, the children switch to a different letter or pass their letters to a peer (whichever is physically easier).
5. At the end, the children finish decorating a letter that was originally started by a peer.
6. The children then glue all the letters on a larger paper to display their work together.
7. The teacher states, "Great job! You all helped each other finish the poster!" Teacher queries: "What did you all do?" Children are prompted to respond, "I helped everyone finish the poster!"

Reinforcers

Children are reinforced with verbal praise, physical praise (high fives, tickles, hugs, pats on the back, sensory input), tangibles (stickers), and positive facial expressions for helping everyone finish the poster.

Week 1 Helps Complete an Activity That Has Been Started
Day 4 Thursday — Five Stations

Materials

- Legos®
- Play dough
- Butcher paper
- Markers
- Craft (e.g., popsicle stick frame to create and decorate)
- Stringing beads
- Bell

Set Up

Teacher sets up 3-5 tables about two feet apart from one another in a row or in a circle. For example, at Station One, there are Legos®; at Station Two, there is play dough; at Station Three, there is butcher paper and markers; at Station Four, there is a craft; and at Station Five, there is a long string with a bowl of beads.

Model the Skill

Teachers A and B model the activity by beginning at one station and then switching to a different station when the bell rings after two minutes. At the Lego® station, Teacher A begins to build something with the Legos®. Teacher B makes something with play dough (starting with a large ball). When the bell rings, they switch: Teacher A adds to Teacher B's play dough, while Teacher B adds to Teacher A's Legos®. The teachers must clarify that the children are to add to the existing project and not destroy or take anything apart.

Guided Lesson

1. Children sit in a circle on the floor.
2. The teacher assigns each child to a station.
3. The teacher reminds the children, "Remember, we are finishing our friends' creations, so you can only add to their project; you cannot take anything apart."
4. The bell rings and children start making something at their station.
5. Children spend two minutes at each station.

6. When the bell rings, children are told to leave their activity and move to the station to their right.

7. At the end, one finished item is produced at each station.

8. The children can hold up the end product and state, "I helped my friends make a ___."

Reinforcers

Children are reinforced with verbal praise, physical praise (high fives, tickles, hugs, pats on the back, sensory input), tangibles (the completed projects, a sticker from one of the activities), and positive facial expressions for helping each other finish creative projects.

Week 1	Helps Complete an Activity That Has Been Started
Day 5	Friday — Puzzle Switch

Materials

- One puzzle per child
- Bell

Model the Skill

Teacher A models the skill by beginning a puzzle, and then switching to Teacher B's puzzle when the bell rings after two minutes.

Guided Lesson

1. Children sit in a circle at the table.
2. Children begin their individual puzzles.
3. Children spend two minutes working on a puzzle.
4. When the bell rings, children switch their puzzles with the child to their right. Teacher can state, "Switch!"
5. At the end, each puzzle is completed.
6. The children can show the teacher the puzzle they completed and state, "I helped my friends finish a puzzle!"

Reinforcers

Children are reinforced with verbal praise, physical praise (high fives, tickles, hugs, pats on the back, sensory input), and positive facial expressions for helping their friends finish a puzzle.

Week 1 **Helps Complete an Activity That Has Been Started**
Generalization Ideas For The Classroom

Generalizing "I Helped You Finish!"

Each of the following activities require one child to start an activity or job, and then have another child complete the task. Prompt the children to identify the fact that they have finished someone else's activity, and encourage using the sentence, 'I helped you finish ___."

- Classroom Jobs: Pick one child to do a job for the first part of the week and have another child finish it for the rest of the week.

- Free Play: Observe children; if they start an activity (e.g., trains, Legos®, blocks) and then move to something else, encourage another child to finish it.

- Circle Time: If there is singing during circle time, instruct half the class to sing the first part of the song, and have the other half finish the rest of it.

- Passing Out Supplies: Choose one child to pass out supplies. Have him/her stop after half of the group has its materials and select another to child to finish. This works for lunch boxes, papers, and art supplies.

Books

- Clarke, Jacqueline A. *Moose's Loose Tooth*. Illus. Bruce McNally. Scholastic, 2003.

- Szekeres, Cyndy. *Suppertime for Frieda Fuzzypaws*. Sterling, 2009.

- Rosen, Michael, and Helen Oxenbury. *We're Going on a Bear Hunt*. Margaret K. McElderry, 2009.

- Kroll, Steven. *The Biggest Snowman Ever*. Illus. Jeni Bassett. Cartwheel Books, 2005.

- Anastasio, Dina. *Big Bird Can Share*. Golden Press, 1985.

Week 2 | Goes Along With an Idea or Action of Peers
"Follow the Leader"

Behavioral Objective

Children will learn to go along with a peer's action or idea.

Identify the Skill Components

- Ability to think of novel ideas/actions
- Ability to express ideas/actions verbally
- Ability to follow directions from a peer
- Ability to pantomime

Lessons and Materials for the Week

Day	Lesson	Materials
Monday	Follow the Leader	Vinyl tunnel, scooter boards, balance beam
Tuesday	Exercises	None
Wednesday	Instruments	Musical instruments
Thursday	Modified Charades	Animal cards
Friday	Dress-Up	Dress-up items

For the Parents

Dear Parents,

This week, our social skill classroom behavior is:

Category 4: Cooperation	
Week 2	Goes Along with an Idea or Action of Peers "Follow the Leader"

Many children have difficulty following an idea or action of a peer and get upset when they are not allowed to do things their way.

Please encourage your child to follow the actions or ideas of another person (ideally, another child). You can turn this into a game by making reference to "follow the leader."

Here are some ways to practice this skill at home:
- During dinnertime, eat your food in a silly way or make a silly noise and encourage your child to do the same.
- When you are walking up the stairs, do so in a different way (backwards, skipping a step) and have your child imitate.
- If your child has a sibling, have the sibling pick a funny way to go to the bathtub (e.g., pretending to swim down the hall) and have your child imitate.
- If your child has a sibling, have the sibling pick a toy and encourage the child to engage in the chosen activity.
- Tell your child that you will go through the grocery store in a particular sequence (fruits, vegetables, milk, cereal) and have your child follow that sequence.

Week 2	**Goes Along With an Idea or Action of Peers**
Day 1	Monday — Follow the Leader

Introduction to the Topic

"This week, we are learning about following our friends and doing what they're doing."

Materials

- Vinyl tunnel
- Scooter boards
- Balance beam (can be constructed by placing wooden blocks on the floor)

Model the Skill

Teacher A tells the children that he/she will pick a funny way to go through the tunnel and that Teacher B will follow. Teacher A goes through the tunnel by crawling on his/her back; Teacher B then goes through the tunnel in the same manner and says, "I followed the leader!"

Guided Lesson

1. Children sit in a row on the floor.
2. One child picks a gross motor item and demonstrates an action on it (e.g., go through, jump over, go under).
3. The other children imitate the same action.
4. Children are prompted to say, "I followed the leader!" when they complete the action.

Reinforcers

Children are reinforced with verbal praise, physical praise (high fives, tickles, hugs, pats on the back, sensory input), tangibles (stickers), and positive facial expressions for following the leader.

Week 2	**Goes Along With an Idea or Action of Peers**
Day 2	Tuesday — Exercises

Materials

- None

Model the Skill

Teacher A does an exercise (e.g., jumping jacks) and Teacher B imitates the same action.

Guided Lesson

1. One child picks an exercise (e.g., running in place).

2. All the other children imitate the same exercise.

3. Children are encouraged to say, "I followed the leader!"

Reinforcers

Children are reinforced with verbal praise, physical praise (high fives, tickles, hugs, pats on the back, sensory input), tangibles (stickers), and positive facial expressions for following the leader.

Week 2	Goes Along With an Idea or Action of Peers
Day 3	Wednesday — Instruments

Materials

- Musical Instruments

Model the Skill

Teacher A plays an instrument in a certain manner and then passes it to Teacher B. Teacher B imitates the action.

Guided Lesson

1. One child plays his/her instrument in a certain way (e.g., shakes it in the air).

2. Children are instructed to "follow the leader" and play their instrument in the exact same way even if the manner of playing isn't relevant to the instrument (e.g., shaking a drum in the air).

3. All of the other children must play their instrument in the same way, regardless of what instrument they have.

4. Children are encouraged to say, "I followed the leader!"

Reinforcers

Children are reinforced with verbal praise, physical praise (high fives, tickles, hugs, pats on the back, sensory input), tangibles (stickers), and positive facial expressions for following the leader and making musical sounds.

Week 2	Goes Along With an Idea or Action of Peers
Day 4	Thursday — Modified Charades

Materials

- Animal Cards

Model the Skill

Teacher A picks a card and pretends to be the animal on that card.
Teacher B imitates Teacher A.

Guided Lesson

1. One child picks a card and pretends to be the animal on the card.
2. All of the other children imitate the child.
3. Children are encouraged to say, "I followed the leader!"

Reinforcers

Children are reinforced with verbal praise, physical praise (high fives, tickles, hugs, pats on the back, sensory input), tangibles (stickers), and positive facial expressions for following the leader.

Week 2	Goes Along With an Idea or Action of Peers
Day 5	Friday — Dress-Up

Materials

- Dress-up items (two of each accessory)

Model the Skill

Teacher A picks a person to dress up as (e.g., firefighter). Both teachers dress up like firefighters. Teacher A acts out something about the dress-up person, like pretending to hose out a fire, climb a ladder, and so forth.

Guided Lesson

1. Children sit in a row in pairs.
2. One child from the pair picks a dress-up accessory (e.g., policeman outfit) and both children dress up in that costume.
3. The child who made the costume selection then acts out a trait of their character (teacher can provide ideas).

Reinforcers

Children are reinforced with verbal praise, physical praise (high fives, tickles, hugs, pats on the back, sensory input), tangibles (stickers), and positive facial expressions for following the leader.

Week 2 | Goes Along With an Idea or Action of Peers
Generalization Ideas For The Classroom

Generalizing "Follow the Leader"

- Transitions: For each transition to and from recess, select one child as leader and have him/her pick a unique way of walking down the hallway (e.g., skipping) and have all of the other children follow the leader.

- Lunch: Have one child pick a silly way of eating lunch or making a silly noise when eating and have all of the other children imitate.

- Recess: Everyday, have a different child pick an activity for recess and have all of the other children follow the leader.

- Clothes: Everyday, have a different child pick a color of clothing that all of the children must wear the following day.

Books

- Lionni, Leo. *Swimmy.* Dragonfly Books, 1973.

- Soman, David, and Jacky Davis. *Ladybug Girl and Bumblebee Boy.* Dial, 2009.

- Shannon, David. *Good Boy Fergus.* The Blue Sky Press, 2006.

- Murphy, Stuart J. *It's About Time!* Illus. John Speirs. HarperCollins, 2005.

Week 3	Listens Without Interrupting While Another Talks

"Zip It"

Behavioral Objective

Children will learn to not interrupt teachers and peers.

Identify the Skill Components

- Ability to control impulsivities
- Language
- Ability to follow directions
- Cognitive capacity to demonstrate patience

Lessons and Materials for the Week

Day	Lesson	Materials
Monday	Three Little Bears	Three Little Bears storybook, play microphone
Tuesday	Stories	Any storybook
Wednesday	Telephone	None
Thursday	Favorite Conversations	None
Friday	Board Game Leader	Various board games

For the Parents

Dear Parents,

This week, our social skill classroom behavior is:

Category 4: Cooperation	
Week 3	Listens Without Interrupting While Another Talks "Zip It"

Many children frequently interrupt their teachers, parents, or other children when they are talking. It is important for us to teach children how to listen to others so he/she will be accepted in social situations.

Please encourage your child to self-regulate their verbal behavior by using the words, "Zip it."

Here are some ways to practice this skill at home:
• Read an entire bedtime story without having your child interrupt you.
• Have each person in the family share about his/her day without any interruptions.
• If the child has a sibling, have the sibling talk about his/her favorite activity without being interrupted by the child.
• At the park, encourage your child to ask his/her peers questions. Have your child listen to the peers' entire responses without interrupting them.

Week 3 Listens Without Interrupting While Another Talks
Day 1 Monday — Three Little Bears

◼ Introduction to the Topic

"This week, we are going to learn how to be quiet when it's someone else's turn to talk."

Materials

- Three Little Bears storybook
- Play microphone

Model the Skill

This is actually a little play. Each child is assigned a role with a simple line. Teacher models speaking into the microphone, reminding the children to "Zip it" (gesture zipping the mouth closed) when someone else is speaking.

Guided Lesson

1. The teacher assigns a role to each child.
2. The lines used are straight from the book (e.g., "Someone's been eating my porridge.").
3. Children are told that when another child has the microphone, everyone has to "Zip it" and listen without interrupting.
4. Children are given turns to stand up with the microphone and say their lines from the book.
5. The teacher is the narrator and helps the children tell the story using the book. The children's ability to say lines is irrelevant. As long as they are using the microphone and talking, all of the others must "Zip it."
6. Children must listen without interrupting while their peers say their parts.

Reinforcers

Children are reinforced with verbal praise, physical praise (high fives, tickles, hugs, pats on the back, sensory input), tangibles (stickers), and positive facial expressions for not interrupting their peers and listening to their presentations.

Week 3	**Listens Without Interrupting While Another Talks**
Day 2	Tuesday — Stories

Materials

- Storybook

Model the Skill

Teacher A tells the children that when someone else is talking, everyone must "Zip it" (use gesture of pretending to zip the mouth). Teacher A tells the students, "Today, we will each tell our friends about a page in this book." Teacher A models talking about what's on the page of his/her book. Teacher B can interrupt and Teacher A will gesture "Zip it." Teacher B will stop talking and sit quietly.

Guided Lesson

1. Children are reminded that when another child is talking, they need to "Zip it" and have their mouths closed and quiet so they can listen.

2. Children are told, "Today, we are going to tell our friends about a page from this book. Do we interrupt our friends when they are talking about the book? NO!" Children then take turns describing one page of the story. (Whether or not their description matches the actual story is irrelevant).

3. Other children are required to wait quietly with a "zipped" mouth. They are reminded with a gesture first and then if necessary, a verbal and physical prompt to keep their mouths zipped.

Reinforcers

Children are reinforced with verbal praise, physical praise (high fives, tickles, hugs, pats on the back, sensory input), tangibles (stickers), and positive facial expressions for not interrupting their peer.

Week 3	Listens Without Interrupting While Another Talks
Day 3	Wednesday — Telephone

Materials

- None

Model the Skill

Teacher A whispers a sentence to Teacher B. Teacher B whispers the sentence to Teacher C. Teacher C says it out loud.

Guided Lesson

1. The teacher starts the game by whispering a fairly long sentence into one child's ear.

2. This child must whisper the same sentence into the next peer's ear.

3. The last child reveals the sentence to the group.

4. The whole class can play, but if possible, form smaller groups of 4-5 children.

5. After the sentence is revealed, ask the children, "Did you interrupt while your friend was talking? Did you 'Zip it' with your mouths?" If someone says no, practice the same activity again.

Reinforcers

Children are reinforced with verbal praise, physical praise (high fives, tickles, hugs, pats on the back, sensory input), tangibles (stickers), and positive facial expressions for not interrupting their peer.

Week 3 Listens Without Interrupting While Another Talks
Day 4 Thursday — Favorite Conversations

Materials

- None

Model the Skill

Teacher A talks about his/her favorite food. After a limited amount of time, Teacher B must reveal what Teacher A talked about.

Guided Lesson

1. Children talk about their favorite toy/food/animal with a partner.
2. After a limited amount of time, children must share what their partner talked about with the entire group.

Reinforcers

Children are reinforced with verbal praise, physical praise (high fives, tickles, hugs, pats on the back, sensory input), tangibles (stickers), and positive facial expressions for not interrupting their peer.

Week 3	Listens Without Interrupting While Another Talks
Day 5	Friday — Board Game Leader

Materials

- Various board games

Model the Skill

Teacher A explains how to play a particular board game to Teacher B. Teacher B is required to wait quietly.

Guided Lesson

1. Children are divided into pairs.
2. One person from each pair explains how to play a particular board game.
3. The other child in the pair must wait quietly.
4. Children switch roles.

Reinforcers

Children are reinforced with verbal praise, physical praise (high fives, tickles, hugs, pats on the back, sensory input), tangibles (stickers), and positive facial expressions for not interrupting their peer.

Week 3 | Listens Without Interrupting While Another Talks
Generalization Ideas For The Classroom

Generalizing "Zip It"

- Daily Conversation: Everyday, have children pick one item from the classroom to talk about to their peers. If a child interrupts their peer, they cannot share an item the following day.

- Lunch or Snack Conversations: Have one child talk about his/her favorite foods without the other children interrupting.

- Monday Conversation: Have children share what they did over the weekend without other children interrupting.

- Calendar: Each day have one child talk about the day, month, or weather, without other children interrupting.

Books

- Taylor, Thomas. *The Noisiest Night.* Oxford University Press, 2007.

- Rosenthal, Amy Krouse, and Tom Lichtenheld. *Duck! Rabbit!* Chronicle Books, 2009.

- Rueda, Claudia. *My Little Polar Bear.* Scholastic Press, 2009.

- Berry, Joy. *Let's Talk About Needing Attention.* Illus. Maggie Smith. Joy Berry Enterprises, 2008.

- Cook, Julia. *My Mouth Is A Volcano!* Illus. Carrie Hartman. National Center for Youth Issues, 2006.

Conclusion

The ideas and lessons in this curriculum may seem simple conceptually but they provide a much-needed, very user-friendly way for teachers to develop appropriate social behaviors in their classrooms. No other guide or curriculum is specifically designed to systematically address the needs of young children by providing developmentally appropriate concepts and instructional language.

In this curriculum, we include lessons that have been actually tried and tested in a treatment/educational environment. The outcomes and feedback have been extremely positive from the families involved as well as the teachers who have learned about the curriculum. The catch phrases, the repetitive instructional techniques, and the short and simple directions and concepts are key components of the curriculum that contribute to its success. Children with autism or developmental disabilities and preschool children understand and generalize these sequenced skills once they spend the week learning a particular concept. Further, the children retain the skills because the catch phrases are so easy for teachers to use beyond the lesson week and for parents to use beyond the school day.

It is important to note that this curriculum is meant to be implemented as one part of an educational plan that involves instruction in cognitive development as well as other domains of social and emotional development. Such areas include, for example, developing friendships, emotion recognition, joint-attention, play, solving social problems, and social skills with peers and in the community. Again, this is why the lessons are short, so that they can be integrated into an already rich curriculum within a classroom without taking too much time—adding a much needed missing part to the other critical components of the instructional day.

We have provided samples and drafts of single weeks of these lessons to families and teachers. We thank them tremendously for their involvement, feedback, and their dedication to these beautiful children. It was their requests that prompted us to develop and publish this curriculum. Community professionals participating in our program have also identified other areas of need, such as activities that focus on dyadic and group engagement of primarily non-verbal or verbally limited children. There are currently no programs available on how to teach these children group participation as they have generally received most of their instruction individually. This would be a needed area to target in the future.

In conclusion, we suspect that a comprehensive program will lead to the strongest outcomes in social behavior. We hope that this curriculum can ease the difficulty many professionals face by providing a simple and user-friendly way to build and enhance their comprehensive programs and increase positive social experiences for children in their classrooms.

References

Achenbach, T. & Rescorla L. (2000) Child Behavior Checklist 1 ½ - 5 years. Achenbach System of Empirically Based Assessment (ASEBA), University of Vermont.

Beck, A. T. (2004). Cognitive therapy of personality disorders, 2nd edition, New York: Guilford Press.

Begun, R. W. (1995) Ready to Use Social Skill Lessons Activities for Grades PreK-K, San Francisco, CA: Jossey Bass Publishers.

Burns, M. K., & Ysseldyke, J. E. (2009). Reported prevalence of evidence-based instructional practices in special education. Journal of Special Education, 43, 3-11.

Chalk, K. & Bizo, L. A. (2004). Specific praise improves on-task behavior and numeracy enjoyment: A study of year 4 pupils engage in the numeracy hour. Educational Psychology in Practice, 20, 335-351.

Douglass Developmental Disabilities Center Curriculum Checklist (2007). New Brunswick, NJ: Douglass Developmental Disabilities Center.

Dweck, C. S. (2000). Self-theories: Their role in motivation, personality, and development, Hove: Psychology Press.

Ellis, A. (1997). The practice of rational emotive behavior therapy, 2nd edition, New York: Springer Publications.

Forness, S. R. & Kavale, K. A. (2000). Emotional or behavioral disorders: Background and current status of the E/BD terminology and definition. Behavioral Disorders, 25, 264-269.

Graham, S., Harris, K. R., & Reid, R. (1992). Developing self-regulated learners. Focus on Exceptional Children, 24, 1-16.

Gresham, F. & Elliot, J. (2005). The Social Skills Rating System (SSRS). Western Psychological Services.

Guglielmo, H., & Tryon, G. (2001). Social skills training in an integrated preschool program. School Psychology Quarterly, 16, 158-175.

Heward, W. L. (1994). Three "low-tech" strategies for increasing the frequency of active student response during group instruction. In R. Gardner III, D. M. Sainato, J. O., Cooper, T. E. Heron, W. L. Heward, J. Eshleman, et al. (Eds.), Behavior analysis in education: Focus on measurably superior instruction, 283-320, Pacific Grove, CA: Brooks/Cole.

Heward, W. L., Gardner, R. I., Cavanaugh, R. A., Courson, F. H., Grossi, T. A., & Barbetta, P. M. (1996). Everyone participates in this class: Using response cards to increase active student responses. Teaching Exceptional Children, 28, 4-10.

Leaf, R. & McEachin, J. (1999). A Work In Progress. New York, NY: DRL Books.

McKinnon, K. & Krempa, K. (2005). Social Skill Solutions: A Hands-On Manual for Teaching Social Skills to Children with Autism. New York, NY: DRL Books.

Moyes, R. A. (2001). Incorporating Social Goals in the Classroom: A Guide for Teachers and Parents of High Functioning Children with Autism and Aspergers Syndrome. Philadelphia, PA: Jessica Kingsley Publishers.

Mueller, M. M., Palkovic, C. M., & Maynard, C. S. (2007). Errorless learning: review and practical application for teaching children with pervasive developmental disorders. Psychology in the Schools, 44, 691-700.

Ozonoff, S., Dawson, G., & McPartland, J. (2002). A Parent's Guide to Asperger Syndrome and High Functioning Autism: How to Meet the Challenges and Help Your Child Thrive, New York, NY: Guilford Press.

Shores, R. E., Gunter, P. L., & Jack, S. L. (1993). Classroom management strategies: Are they setting events for coercion? Behavioral Disorders, 18, 92-102.

VanMeter, L., Fein, D., Morris, R., Waterhouse, L., & Allen, D. (1997). Delay versus deviance in autistic social behavior. Journal of Autism and Developmental Disorders, 27, 557-569.

Notes

Notes

Notes

Notes

Notes